More to the Story

Savoring Details in God's Word

MARK KINKADE

WESTBOW
PRESS®
A DIVISION OF THOMAS NELSON
& ZONDERVAN

WestBow Press books may be ordered through booksellers or by contacting:

WestBow Press
A Division of Thomas Nelson & Zondervan
1663 Liberty Drive
Bloomington, IN 47403
www.westbowpress.com
844-714-3454

ISBN: 978-1-6642-2828-3 (sc)
ISBN: 978-1-6642-2829-0 (hc)
ISBN: 978-1-6642-2830-6 (e)

Library of Congress Control Number: 2021906105

Print information available on the last page.

WestBow Press rev. date: 05/06/2021

Contents

Foreword

Our world is moving at such a rapid rate that it can be easy to miss the beauty of our surroundings and the details that truly matter. The Bible is no exception. Most people read Scripture for a personal devotion in order to glean some kind of encouragement or practical next step. While I want to honor those efforts and the desire to receive encouragement from God's Word, I also think it's important to caution against a casual approach to the Bible. I think we can miss the intention of Scripture by mishandling it.

Look at what the apostle Paul said, to further emphasize this point: "Do your best to present yourself to God as one approved, a worker who has no need to be ashamed, rightly handling the word of truth" (2 Timothy 2:15).

Paul told young Timothy to "study" as a way of presenting himself before God and His holy Word. A faithful and studied approach to God's Word will bring about a more accurate understanding of what was originally meant. If we are to live in obedience to God's Word, then we must first understand what it means.

Friends, let us remember that the Bible is more than a book. The Bible is more than letters on a page that convey good thoughts, historical accounts, great poetry, and a general outline of God's plan. The Bible is God's Word. The way we view and approach the Bible will determine everything regarding our overall spiritual health, which is not something we should take lightly.

I say all of this because it is quite clear that author Mark Kinkade has gone to great lengths to uncover the meaning of many passages of Scripture by carefully pointing out the details that will open your eyes, encourage your heart, and strengthen your faith. This is what it looks like to study the Word in order to bring about its proper meaning, and I believe it will not only give you understanding but also encourage you to dig deeper into the Word for yourself.

Even though I study the Bible daily, I can still miss so many details in Scripture that inform a proper perspective of the text. This is why a book like this is so helpful and why I recommend that you read it and learn to patiently study the Bible in a way that brings the same revelation that you will read throughout *More to the Story*.

Benjamin Dixon
Author of *Hearing God* and *Prophesy*
Lead Pastor of Northwest Church
Federal Way, WA
www.bendixon.org

Introduction

Many of us have read the Bible many times through the years if we have been fortunate enough to have known the Lord for a long time. Unfortunately, many of us have not had the luxury of time to thoroughly mine the verses and stories we read in Scripture. For many years, I have been driven by curiosity to discover the answers to why odd details are recorded in the Bible's pages. It is amazing that even in the most obscure details, God has lessons for His people to learn. I hope to encourage you to read the Bible with fresh eyes and to strengthen your spiritual and practical Christian walk.

Parable of the Two Miners

When it comes to gold mining, two general methods are used. The first relies on the fact that gold is heavy. In this method, water mixed with dirt and gravel is poured down a corrugated ramp. The dirt and gravel all wash away, while the heavy gold particles are caught in the ramp's corrugations. In ancient times, a sheep's fleece was used to catch gold on the ramp, hence the term *Golden Fleece*.

The second method is more mechanical. In this one, the gold-bearing ore is blasted out of the hard rock and excavated by hand or machine. The ore and rocks are then crushed into small pieces and sent to the smelter or refinery. There, intensely hot fires melt the gold out of the ore and burn off any impurities.

The explanation of the parable is this: the gold represents insights and understanding of kingdom principles found in God's Word. The two miners represent the people of God, and the miner picking up a nugget can be anyone — a new believer or you or me. The Holy Spirit freely gives understanding and insights of God's Word. Progressively, as more and more complex tools are used, the believer is required to spend study time and prayer seeking to understand the Word. The hard-rock miner corresponds to spiritual leaders, pastors, or teachers, who are trained to understand original biblical languages and the use of research tools in order to glean insights.

It is important to note that these gold nuggets of spiritual insight are of equal value to all people—saved and unsaved alike. More remarkable is that, in sharing spiritual gold, the one receiving the gold is richer without making the giver any less rich!

The apostle Paul encouraged believers to share with their leaders in Galatians 6:6: "Let the one who is taught the word share all good things with the one who teaches."

Paul is talking about physical provision, but the principle regarding spiritual things is true for all concerned. My purpose in this book is to share insights and discoveries with the reader, and I delight to receive insights in return.

Share your gold at mark.kinkade.author@outlook.com.

Chapter 1

Friends of God

In John 15:15, Jesus said,

> No longer do I call you servants, for the servant does not know what his master is doing; but I have called you friends, for all that I have heard from my Father I have made known to you.

For most people, grammar is near if not at the top of their "most boring" list. However, at times, considering the grammar of what and how something is said is insightful. So have patience as we explore the details of the above verse.

The form of the word *call* in the beginning of this verse in the original Greek is present indicative active tense, which indicates that Jesus is no longer calling (that is, continuously calling) them servants. However, the second use of the word is in the perfect tense, which means the action was performed in the past with continuing consequences. The action is summarized and presented in its entirety. An English analogy is, "He loosed the arrow." The perfect tense is considered by many to be a third type of aspect (perfect or stative) that focuses on a state that arises from a previous action. This is complicated Greek grammar, but here is how it breaks down: Jesus is saying that, at some time in the past, He called us friends even though He was also calling us servants (Greek – slaves). He was a friend to the slave.

The real surprise is this: since the members of the Trinity are in complete unity (John 10:30), Jesus and the Father are one. Then, by implication, *each member of the Trinity calls us friends!*

Now that we realize that each member of the Trinity considers us friends, let us consider what this or any friendship means.

1. The apostle Paul said bad company corrupts good morals (1 Corinthians 15:33). The converse of this statement is good company enhances good morals or character. This principle is hinted at in Romans 12:2.

   > Do not be conformed to this world, but be transformed by the renewal of your mind, that by testing you may discern what is the will of God, what is good and acceptable and perfect.

   And Hebrews 10:24–25 says,

   > And let us consider how to stir up one another to love and good works, not neglecting to meet together, as is the habit of some, but encouraging one another, and all the more as you see the Day drawing near.

2. In everyday life, friendships are strengthened through conversation, activities, and spending time together. So,

naturally proceeding from the previous concept, intentionally spending time with each member of the Trinity enhances your friendship as well as your character and morals. Practically speaking, this is not limited to your quiet time and Bible study. How about considering inviting your friends along to enjoy mundane, secular activities with you? A whole new level of intimate friendship is possible when doing chores, working at your job, playing sports, or spending time with your spouse. Jesus defined *love* in terms of a friend's sacrifice in John 15:13: "Greater love has no one than this, that someone lay down his life for his friends."

If we think about it, we will see that God is intimately interested in every aspect of our individual lives.

Finally, Jesus said, "I have called you friends." This *have called* raises an additional question. To whom was he talking? It does not make sense that it was the disciples since this appears to be new information for them. (Jesus did not say, "You remember me telling you …") Why would he phrase it this way unless it was to remind or inform them of something he had said previously? A surprising alternative could very well be that it was part of the conversation occurring from the foundation of the world, as referenced in Matthew 25:34.

> Then the King will say to those on his right, "Come, you who are blessed by my Father, inherit the kingdom prepared for you from the foundation of the world."

Ephesians 1:4 says,

Even as he chose us in him before the foundation of the world, that we should be holy and blameless before him.

And Revelation 13:8 adds,

And all who dwell on earth will worship it, everyone whose name has not been written before the foundation of the world in the book of life of the Lamb who was slain.

We certainly know there was a conversation from Genesis 1:26.

Then God said, "Let us make man in our image, after our likeness. And let them have dominion over the fish of the sea and over the birds of the heavens and over the livestock and over all the earth and over every creeping thing that creeps on the earth."

From this verse and the many instances of Jesus talking to the Father, we see that communication is inherently part of the divine community and may very well be part of being created in God's image. This proclamation of friendship may have occurred in the divine community before the time of Genesis 1:1. Such is the magnitude of the Trinity's love and friendship toward us!

Lesson

Friendship is usually a two-way affair. However, in God's case, He loved us while we were sinners and estranged. Now that we accept Jesus as our personal Savior, the sky is the limit as to how rich and rewarding the friendship can be.

Questions for Pondering

Are there any areas in my life I would be uncomfortable inviting my Trinitarian friends to enjoy with me?

If so, why? What am I going to do about it?

Am I being honest with these friends? They already know all my secrets!

Chapter 2

Aaron's Blessing Plural

> The LORD bless you and keep you; the LORD make his face(s) to shine upon you and be gracious to you; the LORD lift up his countenance(s) (smile) upon you and give you peace. —Numbers 6:24–26

In the Hebrew, *face* and *countenance* are represented by the same word—*pâniym,* which is in the plural form. In the New Testament, we learned that the Trinity is one God in three persons. This is implied in the Old Testament but not understood. Since *pâniym* is a plural word, wouldn't it make sense that each member of the Trinity desires to be an active participant in blessing people? So, it might be better translated as, "The LORD bless you and keep you; the LORD make his *faces* to shine upon you and be gracious to you; the LORD lift up his *countenances* upon you and give you peace" (emphasis added).

This would be in keeping with an understanding of friendship with a God who loves and desires to do good for His friends. God has plans for us, even in desperate times.

Jeremiah 29:11 says,

> For I know the plans I have for you, declares the Lord,
> plans for welfare and not for evil, to give you a future
> and a hope.

Lesson

These plans of God stem from his boundless agape love, which blesses
and acts for the recipients' best interest, even if the recipients do not
view it as such. It is much like a parent taking a young child to the
doctor for an immunization. The young child would rather *not* get
poked with the needle, but it is good for the child.

Questions for Pondering

This blessing was given at the specific direction of God Himself.
Since each member of the Trinity has a personality, what might the
blessing stemming from each member look like?

How might their individual blessings be similar?

How might their individual blessing differ?

Chapter 3

God's Library

Most Christians are familiar with or at least have heard of the Lamb's Book of Life mentioned in the Bible. However, have you ever thought about God's other books mentioned in Scripture? The following are the significant references to these books:

- Psalm 69:28 (a possible reference to the Lamb's Book of Life!): "Let them be blotted out of the book of the living; let them not be enrolled among the righteous."
- Psalm 139:16: "Your eyes saw my unformed substance; in your book were written, every one of them, the days that were formed for me, when as yet there was none of them."
- Daniel 7:10 (from the vision about the Ancient of Days): "A stream of fire issued and came out from before him; a thousand thousands served him, and ten thousand times ten thousand stood before him; the court sat in judgment, and the books were opened."
- Daniel 10:21 (the book of truth): "But I will tell you what is inscribed in the book of truth: there is none who contends by my side against these except Michael, your prince."

- Malachi 3:16 (the book of remembrance): "Then those who feared the LORD spoke with one another. The LORD paid attention and heard them, and a book of remembrance was written before him of those who feared the LORD and esteemed his name."
- Revelation 20:12 (the Last Judgment scene): "And I saw the dead, great and small, standing before the throne, and books were opened. Then another book was opened, which is the book of life. And the dead were judged by what was written in the books, according to what they had done."
- Micah 7:19 is figurative language, but is it putting the books or memory of their record in an inaccessible place? "He will again have compassion on us; he will tread our iniquities underfoot. You will cast all our sins into the depths of the sea."

As you can see from the above references, God indeed has a formidable library! Have you considered what the purpose of such a library would be, especially since God is omniscient (all-knowing)? Obviously, it is not for God's benefit. So, for whose benefit would such books be written? The likely answer is that they are for us and the angelic host. It is an established fact that in today's contract-dependent society, many have discovered to their sorrow that it is hard to argue against what is accurately written down.

Lesson

The opportunity for review is a strong argument for the practice of daily journaling. Reviewing old journals or diaries will help you recall events and memories long forgotten. One such instance is recorded in Esther 2:21ff and Esther 5:14—6:10, where Mordecai reports to the king on a plot against his life and Mordecai was never rewarded. This detail is discovered when the king reads some of his old journals. In this instance, God used this practice to spare Mordecai's life from Haman's plot to kill him.

Questions for Pondering

What might you discover if you reviewed some of your old journals?

If you have not kept journals, how about reviewing old Bible study notes?

Finally, why not write down memories of times when God has been significantly active in your life? Collaborate with others who were participants or observers in these instances to document the details you may have forgotten.

In all these notes, seek the Lord to show you lessons for today or insights in whatever endeavor He has called you to in this season of your life.

Chapter 4

When God Sought to Kill Moses!

At a lodging place on the way the LORD met him and sought to put him to death. Then Zipporah took a flint and cut off her son's foreskin and touched Moses' feet with it and said, "Surely you are a bridegroom of blood to me!" So, he let him alone. It was then that she said, "A bridegroom of blood," because of the circumcision. (Exodus 4:24–26)

Have you ever wondered about this story? God has commissioned Moses to free his people from slavery in Egypt. Out of nowhere, we are told that, on the way, God seeks to kill him! There seems to be something odd going on here. First of all, many English translations put in Moses' name here, but in the Hebrew text the pronouns *him* and *his* are used. Just who is being referenced to is ambiguous. It could mean Moses, but could also mean his son.[1] Due to the ambiguity of the pronoun use, much is left unsaid. If it was the son, then why did Zipporah perform the circumcision and not Moses? Therefore, it is most likely that it is Moses who is being attacked. In Jewish thought, it is the Angel of the LORD who is attacking and thus allowing Zipporah to see what is happening and take action. It is unclear as to the form of the attack, but it was likely an illness of some form. This would allow time enough for her to get a knife and perform the ceremony. Her remark in verse 26 reveals that she was at odds with Moses in this matter. It appears that both boys are young, since Zipporah and both boys are riding one donkey, see verse 20.

Could it be that Moses sends his family back to Jethro at this time because the boy needs to heal and cannot travel the rest of the way to Egypt? Eliezer, the second-born, is not mentioned until Exodus 18:1–4:

> Jethro, the priest of Midian, Moses' father-in-law, heard of all that God had done for Moses and for Israel his people, how the LORD had brought Israel out of Egypt. Now Jethro, Moses' father-in-law, had taken Zipporah, Moses' wife, after he had sent her home, along with her two sons. The name of the one was Gershom (for he said, "I have been a sojourner in a foreign land"), and the name of the other, Eliezer (for he said, "The God of my father was my help, and delivered me from the sword of Pharaoh").

One possibility for not mentioning him is that the death plague was only against the firstborn, see verse 23. This would account for only one son being mentioned in the Hebrew text. Another possibility is that Eliezer was already circumcised. Notice that Eliezer's name references being delivered from the sword of Pharaoh. This may be a reference from Moses' escape forty years earlier.

Alternately, he could have sent her back to her father later with the news noted above. This seems unlikely since she would have to go both ways with her sons. If Moses' purpose was to send Jethro news of Israel's deliverance, sending a messenger with the report makes more sense.

This incident occurs after Moses' encounter with I AM at the burning bush. Jethro would of course know of Moses' mission and may very well have learned about the plagues from trade caravans or travelers. News of these miraculous signs and wonders in Egypt would have been exciting to those in the surrounding regions. What is clear is that Moses sends Zipporah and the two sons back to Jethro at some point. The time frame between chapters 4 and 18 is never specified, but it appears that Moses' family is not with him when he confronts Pharaoh. It is possible that only a few months pass, but it could feasibly be a year or more.

From the text of this story, Gershon is not circumcised because of Zipporah's opposition. Somehow she understands that Moses' (or her son's) life is in jeopardy because of the failure to circumcise her son. Although Abraham's son, Midian, is circumcised—because Abraham would have kept covenant—there is no record to indicate that the Midianite people practiced this custom.

The question still remains, Why would God seek to kill Moses because one of his sons is not circumcised? It appears that this dispute in Moses and Zipporah's marriage has arisen over whether or not to circumcise the son. Zipporah is against Moses in this matter. As a result of Zipporah's insistence, Moses demonstrated a failure in leadership. But God is very clear about the details of the Abrahamic covenant.

The sign of the covenant is circumcision. The covenant is traced through the descendants of Sarah (Genesis 15), not through the descendants of Keturah, Abraham's second wife (Genesis 25). In the verses immediately preceding this incident, God has told Moses to tell Pharaoh that if he will not let God's firstborn nation (Israel) go, God will kill Pharaoh's firstborn son. In view of this detail, it likely follows that it is Gershom (Moses' firstborn) who is being attacked because he is not part of the covenant people.

> Both he who is born in your house and he who is bought with your money, shall surely be circumcised. So shall my covenant be in your flesh an everlasting covenant. Any uncircumcised male who is not circumcised in the flesh of his foreskin shall be cut off from his people; he has broken my covenant. (Genesis 17:13–14)

There is another issue in this story that involves a principle explained in the New Testament. This issue also is critical. Moses has a leadership failure in his family. The apostle Paul enumerates qualifications for leadership in the church. He asks how someone who does not know how to manage his own household will care for God's church?

> He must manage his own household well, … for if someone does not know how to manage his own household, how will he care for God's church? (1 Timothy 3:4–5)

Therefore, if Moses is not managing his household well, how then can he be expected to manage the responsibility of leading the nation?

God is holy, faithful, and loving and therefore deals with the whole family. All at once He has helped Moses' leadership, taught Zipporah submission, and brought the son into the covenant.

Lesson

There are at least two lessons at least in these verses.

1. Prior to the birth, death, and resurrection of Jesus, circumcision of flesh was the sign of the Abrahamic covenant, but now, looking through the lens of the cross, the circumcision of the heart (Jeremiah 31:33, Deuteronomy 30:6) is the new rule for the sign of the covenant. This is the "being born of God" referred to in John 1:12 and being "born again" in John 3:3.

2. In God's sovereignty and omniscience, He can work in one area of a person's life to achieve multiple purposes that can affect multiple people. An example of this, often seen in hindsight, is the death of a loved one, even though we prayed for their healing. We may get angry at God for not answering our prayers as we asked, while the testimony of our loved one's faith while facing death results in the salvation of someone looking on.

Questions for Pondering

Have I entered into this new covenant relationship with Jesus by

1. repenting of my sin;
2. asking Him to forgive me;
3. accepting His vicarious death and resurrection for me personally;
4. committing my life to follow and obey His commands;
5. walking humbly with Him, depending on His help to overcome life's problems; and
6. accepting His sovereign will in my life knowing He has the best interests in mind for all His people?

If you desire to do these steps, then here is a sample prayer:

Dear Jesus, I acknowledge that I have broken your Commandments and followed my own rebellious ways.

I believe Jesus of Nazareth is the Son of God.
I believe that He died on a cross for my sins.
I believe He was raised to life again for my justification.
Almighty God forgive me of my sins—I forgive all who have sinned against me.
Jesus, I turn from my old ways. Be Lord of my life, Lord of all that I have, Lord of all that I am, Lord of all that I will ever be. I will serve You with my whole heart, mind, soul, and body—amen.

Next steps:

- Get water baptized to physically confess you have died with Jesus and will rise with Him to new life.
- Ask Father God to fill you with the Holy Spirit for His service.
- Read the Gospel of John to better understand what the Christian life is all about.
- Find a Bible believing church to help you grow as you walk in this new life with Jesus as your king.

Chapter 5

Why a Box in Heaven?

Much has been taught about the tabernacle Moses had constructed in the wilderness after the Exodus. But have you ever wondered about Exodus 25:8–10, where God instructs Moses to build an ark and furniture exactly according to the pattern he was shown? In Hebrews 8:5 and 9:23, we are told that the items in the earthly tabernacle were replicas of what was in heaven.

To look at the ark of the covenant, you would think it is simply a box with a lid overlaid with gold. But we are given two details of interest surrounding its purpose. The first is that God tells Moses He will meet with him from above "the mercy seat," or lid of the ark of the covenant. This implies that the lid is God's earthly throne. Surprise! This box is a replica of the one in God's holy temple, as stated in Revelation 11:19. This leads to two questions:

1. Is the heavenly temple normally closed and restricted, as was the earthly counterpart?
2. Why is there a "box" in heaven?

The first question we may deal with later. Now, the ark of the covenant was the repository of the Book of the Law or covenant, and maybe also of all the other books in God's library.

This leads to a second detail of interest. Namely, life is in the blood, and it speaks. In Abel's case in Genesis 4:10, the blood cried for vengeance, but for the ark of the earthly tabernacle, the high priest sprinkles the blood of atonement on the mercy seat once a year. For the ark found in God's temple, according to Hebrews 9:12, the blood is Jesus', and this blood speaks of forgiveness. So, in this case, the blood is there to stop anyone from lifting the lid and looking at the library recounting His people's sins. In Isaiah 38:17 and 43:25, the blood serves a different purpose. The Hebrew phrase *blots out* here does not refer to covering or atoning but to erasing, as in washing or rubbing out. This is reminiscent of the blood of Jesus washing us white as snow in Isaiah 1:16–18 and again in Revelation 7:14.

The imagery in Isaiah 38:17 is quite interesting. If God is sitting on His throne (mercy seat), then putting it "behind His back" is a metaphor for putting it in the box. The net result is that, in order to open the box to get at the library, one must get past the living blood of Jesus, our High Priest, *and* one must dethrone God! This is *not* going to happen!

This is the library that will never be read again!

Lesson

We are all so sin conscious that it is hard at times for us to believe in our forgiveness. God knows we need extra encouragement, so among the many verses of encouragement telling us He does not remember our sins, He repeats it twice in Psalm 103:3 and Psalm 103:11–12.

Questions for Pondering

Have I allowed my sin consciousness to hinder my relationship and fellowship with the Lord?

Do I believe what God has said, or have I allowed Satan to get me to doubt?

Chapter 6

Swimming Pigs

Most everyone is familiar with the story of the deliverance of the Gerasene man found in Mark 5:2, 6–8. This demonized man came running and fell down before Jesus, pleading Him not to torment him. Jesus asked him his name, to which he replied, "Legion," for there were many demons. The Greek grammar here is interesting. Jesus asked his name when He discovered resistance to His command that the demons come out of the man. The Greek tense of the word implies a continuous act of commanding. The demons pleaded for Him not to send them out of the country but to be permitted to enter a herd of about three thousand pigs. They did, and the herd ran down the hill into the Galilean sea and drowned.

There are a number of unusual things about this story. First, it is apparent that the aggregate of gathered demons had a limited ability to resist Jesus' command. Second, why did Jesus grant the demonic request? The answer may lie in realizing that Jesus was very intentional in all He did. The immediate result of the death of the swine herd got the attention and fear of the owners. Resulting in their begging Jesus to leave. Now that the man is free, he stays and witnesses his deliverance to the people of the Decapolis region, see verse 20. Later, when Jesus returns to the Decapolis area, He is welcomed.

The most perplexing detail of this incident is that the pigs drowned. In case you did not know, pigs are excellent swimmers! So, there must be more to the story. Let's analyze the facts. The definition of *legion* says that the word originated as the main division of the Roman army and comprised between four thousand and six thousand men. It was divided into ten cohorts and these in turn into six centuries each. Sometimes a small cavalry division of about 120 was attached,[2] plus auxiliaries. So conservatively, a legion comprised between 4,000 and 6,800 men. In the case of this story, that many demons were all dwelling in one man. In the conversation with Jesus, one demon seems to be speaking, and he calls himself Legion, implying the presence of a spirit of superior power in addition to subordinate ones.[3]

In several places, Scripture records that the believer is the temple where the Holy Spirit dwells. So, we see that one human being can contain the Holy Spirit or over six thousand demons, yet three thousand pigs went insane with an average of one to two demons possessing each one of them and drowned. It is no wonder that the psalmist declares we are indeed fearfully and wonderfully made—to have intimate fellowship with the Holy Trinity!

Lesson

It has been said that each individual person is like a house, composed of rooms, closets, and secret places corresponding to areas in his or her life. When we invite Jesus to be our Savior, He sends the Holy Spirit to take up residence. As we grow in our intimate relationship with the Trinity, we turn over more and more of our life to Him.

Question for Pondering

Like rooms in a house, are there areas in my life that I have kept locked and denied access or control to my Savior?

Chapter 7

Christ, the Prime Initiator

The greatest minds in physics are constantly working on the grand theory that would unify Einstein's theory of relativity (which explains how things behave on the large scale we can see) with quantum mechanics (which explains how the unseen world of atomic particles and light behave). For example, quantum mechanics explains how light acts like both a wave and a particle—bends to create color from a prism or reflect as in a mirror. This grand theory is known as the theory of everything (TOE).[4] The current working theory is known as string theory, where incredibly small, vibrating strings determine all the many kinds of subatomic particles that comprise the world we see. The strings vary in length and energy, causing them to vibrate at different rates. All these variables determine the makeup of every particle, big or small. One such particle is the light particle called a photon, the first thing created as recorded in Genesis 1:3. The Bible has several other references to God's creation of the universe.

> By the word of the LORD the heavens were made, and
> by the breath of his mouth all their host. (Psalm 33:6)

In the beginning was the Word, and the Word was with God, and the Word was God. He was in the beginning with God. All things were made through him, and without him was not anything made that was made. (John 1:1-3)

He (Jesus Christ) is the radiance of the glory of God and the exact imprint of his nature, and he upholds the universe by the word of his power. After making purification for sins, he sat down at the right hand of the Majesty on high. (Hebrews 1:3)

This last verse is intriguing to a physicist, especially the phrase "by the word of His power." In the original Greek language, *word* is *rhema*, which can mean "utterance." In relating this phrase to string theory from the above TOE, the Genesis account of creation relates repeatedly that "God said...." Additionally, a related passage is Colossians 1:16, which states that all things visible and invisible were created by Christ and are held together by Him.

A fascinating meditation point is that the voice of Jesus Christ (the prime initiator) at creation started all the various strings in motion. In the beginning (Genesis 1:1), He created all the strings. The strings, although not vibrating, represent the existence of all creation. God conceived of creation and us before the foundation of the earth. When He speaks, the strings start moving to create the things mentioned on each day of creation. This theory provides an intriguing insight on creation. If the universe is indeed composed of these ultrasmall strings, then how amazing to have Moses express creation in terms of speaking things into existence and thus setting these strings into motion. Moses wrote all this some four thousand years before Einstein and company were even born.

Lesson

An axiom to consider is that one must conceive and plan before execution, just as an architect draws up blueprints before construction of the building begins.

Questions for Pondering

God declared in Genesis 11:6,

> And the LORD said, "Behold, they are one people, and they have all one language, and this is only the beginning of what they will do. And nothing that they propose to do will now be impossible for them."

> And Jesus said to him, "'If you can'! All things are possible for one who believes." (Mark 9:23)

> I can do all things through him who strengthens me. (Philippians 4:13)

The big question, then, is what do I imagine?

- Am I dreaming too small?
- Are my dreams and plans very big?
- How much bigger can my dreams and plans become if I depend on the Lord?

Chapter 8

Jacob and Esau: Blessing without Deception

Have you ever been bothered by Jacob's deception to get the firstborn blessing? It seems Jacob took the law into his own hands. What seems to be often overlooked is who else was operating in disobedience. Prior to the twins' birth, Rebekah inquired of the LORD why the children struggled within her womb. The LORD's response was a prophecy that two nations were in her womb and the older would serve the younger (Genesis 25:23).

This prophecy is shocking, considering the culture where the firstborn had the privilege of the inheritance, leadership, and blessing. And it is unlikely that Isaac would have been ignorant of the LORD's prophecy to his wife. When it came time for the twins to be born, they were named based on physical characteristics. Esau was covered with thick, red hair, and the name *Esau* is a variant of the Arabic word for "hairy." As Esau was being born, the other twin reached out and grabbed Esau's heel, so he was called Jacob, which translates as "heel grabber" or "cheat." One wonders if the above prophecy influenced the naming of Jacob, as generally it was the father who named the children.

Later in the twins' story, we find Esau returning from hunting, faint from hunger and despising his birthright. He trades the birthright to Jacob in exchange for a bowl of red lentil stew. Is it possible that both men knew of their birth prophecy? It would seem probable that Rebekah, at least, would have told the story to the boys. Since this is likely, is it conceivable that Jacob made this deal with this prophecy in mind?

It is not recorded how old they were when this incident occurred, but we know that they were old enough to hunt and cook. It is recorded that they were forty when Esau married (Genesis 26:34). Isaac would have been at least a hundred years old (Genesis 25:26) and likely suffered from cataracts, leaving him blind, though he could see light and dark (dim). From the text we know that Isaac and Rebekah had been married at least sixty years since she was barren for twenty years and Esau married at forty. What would have happened in the following hypothetical situations?

- Rebekah went in to Isaac, when (or even after) Isaac stated his intention to bless Esau, and reminded them both of the LORD's prophecy.
- Rebekah reminded Isaac after Esau had left (if she knew of the incident) that Esau has sold his birthright to Jacob.
- The LORD hindered Esau, preventing him from hunting success, or spoke directly to Isaac to remind him of the prophecy.

The story may well have played out quite differently! The flow of events reveals a character flaw of deception that runs in the family. It seems Rebekah shared a deceptive bent with her brother Laban, who deceived Jacob at least ten times regarding marriage to Rachel and Jacob's wages (Genesis 31:41). Jacob learned his deceitful behavior from his mother. The future grief and consequences for Jacob and Rebekah were severe indeed. Jacob was separated from his family and deceived multiple times by Laban. Rebekah's deception causes Jacob to flee Esau's wrath, so she was not allowed to see her son for twenty years, during which time she may have died since the time of her death is not recorded. (Note that she takes on the curse for Jacob's deception—Genesis 27:13.) Esau also was party to deception since he knew full well that he sold his blessing and birthright to Jacob (Genesis 27:36).

Lesson

God is self-sufficient and does not require our help. Jesus taught that if one seeks first the kingdom of God, then all one's needs will be provided (Matthew 6:33).

Questions for Pondering

With God's promise of care, what answers to prayer might I expect?

Have I been deceptive or manipulated situations or people to get what I wanted in my job or relationships?

What am I continuing to trust the Lord for in order to get my heart's desire or see what I have prayed for come to pass?

Chapter 9

Joseph Sent to Prison Instead of Being Executed

Genesis chapter 39 recounts the story of Joseph being sold into slavery. As a slave sold to Potiphar, Joseph has God's blessing. Potiphar recognizes Joseph's skill and blessing and places all he has into Joseph's stewardship (Genesis 39:2–4).

Over time, Potiphar's wife entices Joseph, who is a handsome young man. Joseph's integrity leads him to reject her advances, honoring Potiphar and giving glory to God (Genesis 39:9). Finally, one day he is trapped, and the rejected woman falsely accuses Joseph. The text says that as soon as Potiphar heard his wife's accusation, his anger was kindled (Genesis 39:11–19). The surprising result is that Potiphar has Joseph put in prison rather than having him executed.

The key to this apparent discrepancy is in asking with whom is Potiphar angry. Normally, we would assume that he is angry at Joseph, but there is another possibility. The text says that, from the time Joseph became his steward, all that Potiphar had in house and field prospered. Potiphar had time to get to know Joseph and to assess his character.

Likewise, he also must know his wife and her character, so he may have been angry at his wife. Recognizing his wife's ploy against Joseph, perhaps Potiphar sends Joseph to jail to protect him from his wife's revenge. If his anger was directed against Joseph, he would have had him, as his slave, executed or, worse, tortured. In prison, Joseph again gains favor.

> But the LORD was with Joseph and showed him steadfast love and gave him favor in the sight of the keeper of the prison. And the keeper of the prison put Joseph in charge of all the prisoners who were in the prison. Whatever was done there, he was the one who did it. (Genesis 39:21–22)

If a prisoner loses favor and is to be punished, he would be restrained in irons and put in the worst cell. How then could Joseph gain favor with the jailer? If Potiphar's anger was directed at his wife, then the only way he could have protected Joseph would be to sequester him away from his wife's vindictiveness. One then wonders what conversation Potiphar had (at the LORD's design) with the keeper of the prison. Since Potiphar is the captain of the guard, it is likely that he also had oversight of this prison.

It is not much of a stretch of the imagination to consider that Potiphar put in a good word on Joseph's behalf.

Lesson

In his immaturity, Joseph flaunted his dreams before his brothers and parents. Over time he had opportunity to ponder these dreams; this, coupled with his humiliation as a slave, shaped his attitude toward honor and leadership.

All of this took time. Joseph remained in prison for two years after interpreting the butler's dream and probably was a slave for at least ten years (Genesis 41:46). Joseph was likely still a teenager when his brothers hatched their plan to sell him into slavery and an older teen when Jacob gave him the robe of many colors as a commemoration of his coming of age. Joseph demonstrated a lack of maturity, even at seventeen, in bringing a bad report against the concubine sons of Bilhah and Zilpah (Dan, Naphtali, Gad, and Asher—Genesis 37:2). Joseph again showed his immaturity later in his retelling of his dreams to his brothers and parents. Joseph's years of hardship must have shaped his attitude given the hope provided in his dreams.

Questions for Pondering

What impact does my attitude have on my situation?

Can a change in attitude change my circumstances?

What am I to be doing in the waiting time for my prayers to be answered?

Am I to grumble and murmur, living in resignation and acceptance, or persevere to continue in prayer and praise to the Lord, trusting in God's faithfulness?

Chapter 10

Ishmael: "Wild Donkey of a Man"

The story of Abraham, Sarah, and Hagar is complicated. When viewed from Ishmael's perspective, it unveils some very revealing surprises! We are all familiar with God's promise that Abraham would have a son by Sarah, through whom God's covenant promises would be fulfilled. But the story shows Sarah being impatient, and she convinces Abraham to beget the promised child through Hagar, her personal slave (Genesis 15:2–4, 16:3–4). So after Abraham had lived ten years in the land of Canaan, Sarah took Hagar, the Egyptian servant, and gave her to Abram as a wife. And he went in to Hagar, and she conceived. And when Hagar saw that she had conceived, she looked with contempt on her mistress.

Hagar has Ishmael, who is thirteen by the time Isaac is born to Sarah (Genesis 16:16, 17:17). By ancient Semitic custom, Isaac was likely weaned after one to three years, making Ishmael fourteen to seventeen years old (Genesis 17:25). By this time Ishmael would have come of age, seeing that he is supplanted as firstborn and mocks Isaac (Genesis 21:9, Galatians 4:28–29). Sarah sees this and demands

Abraham send away (literally "drive out") Hagar and Ishmael from their midst. However, before Ishmael was born, when Hagar was running away from Sarai, Hagar was promised her son would be blessed and be a "wild donkey of a man" (Genesis 16:12). So just what does this statement mean? The wild donkey is described in Job 39:5–8:

> Who has let the wild donkey go free? Who has loosed
> the bonds of the swift donkey, to whom I have given the
> arid plain for his home and the salt land for his dwelling
> place? He scorns the tumult of the city; he hears not the
> shouts of the driver. He ranges the mountains as his
> pasture, and he searches after every green thing.

The wild donkey is known for being swift (outrunning most horses), self-sufficient (able to live in arid country), wily (avoiding populated areas), stubborn (very difficult or impossible to herd), and hardy (makes mountainous terrain its habitat).[5]

The Bible states where the descendants of Ishmael settled in Genesis 25:17–18. The regions from Havilah to Shur correspond to Sinai and northwest Arabia.[6] The Bedouin and Arab people who inhabit the arid and semiarid regions of Sinai and Arabia are a proud, independent, and self-sufficient people, an interesting parallel to the description of the wild donkey above.

Lesson

Has there been a time where you did not get the reward or recognition you thought you deserved at church, school, work, or home? What you do and how you react to events of this nature will impact your character.

Questions for Pondering

How has lack of recognition or reward affected you? Can you look back and see the intervention by the Lord in these situations and recognize it working out for your good?

Chapter 11

Ishmael: "Father Wounds"

With Ishmael's father sending him and his mother away without an inheritance (Genesis 21:14–21), Ishmael experienced resentment and a "father wound." This attitude impacted his character. This feeling or attitude is also known as an orphan mindset.

The orphan mindset says,

- I must achieve, perform, and prove myself since I am on my own;
- I must earn my way into the family to be accepted;
- I do not belong here, so I must be someone I am not;
- I have been rejected or abandoned or do not know who my father is, and I do not know if I have an inheritance;
- Since I do not have an inheritance, I must claw and grab for everything I can get;
- I have no one who looks out for me (a true friend); and
- I particularly aim at taking what belongs to sons since they did not do anything to deserve what they have.

If nurtured, the resentment often leads to anger and, in the worst cases, revenge. It appears that this negative reaction did not impact his character later in life. As a teenager, Ishmael cried under a bush in the wilderness and simply indicated that he was having a pity party. There is no record of violence or animosity toward either Abraham or Isaac. On the contrary, the Bible records his participation with Isaac in burying his father, Abraham (Genesis 25:9).

If there was any resentment, Ishmael would likely not have participated in burying his father. So it is likely that the brothers were on speaking terms and the wounds had healed.

Lesson

When bad things happen to us, we can stay where we are in self pity and perish, or we can get up, move on, and allow the LORD to work things out. Ishmael got up, moved on, married, and was blessed.

Questions for Pondering

Have I allowed circumstances to dictate my path in life?

Have I avoided telling God about my problems but told my problems about my God?

Chapter 12

The Oddity of Jesus Escaping Nazareth Unscathed

The background of this story is Jesus' reading the Isaiah scroll in the synagogue of His hometown, Nazareth. He proclaimed that prophets were sent to Gentiles too, at which time the citizens were incensed, drove Him out of the synagogue, and attempted to throw Him off the cliff near the town. The text says He escaped by passing through their midst (as if invisible) and left town. (Luke 4:22–30)

The key to understanding this odd story is found in just a few preceding verses at the temptation of Jesus:

> Then the devil took him to the holy city and set him on the pinnacle of the temple and said to him, "If you are the Son of God, throw yourself down, for it is written, 'He will command his angels concerning you,' and 'On their hands they will bear you up, lest you strike your foot against a stone.'" (Matthew 4:5–6)

Satan tempts Jesus by misquoting Psalm 91:11–12, deleting the phrase "in all your ways" from the end of verse 11. Why was Satan careful to omit this from his quote of the promise of these verses? To answer this question, we need to investigate just what this phrase means. The main thrust of the verses is God sending angels to guard us from direct satanic murder, or "accidents," and to assist us when we are walking in the path of righteousness. (God cannot condone actions of evil or sin or in disobedience to what He is asking you to do. See the book of Jonah.) Note an angel encouraged Paul in the shipwreck account of Acts 27.

In the Nazareth incident, Jesus is about the Father's business declaring the good news, thus meeting the criteria for the promise of Psalm 91. Scrolls are read sequentially since it is cumbersome to jump to another passage by rerolling. Jesus gets up for this Sabbath in time to read this portion and declares the passage's fulfillment in Himself. The people think well of Him until He points out that God cares not only for the Jew but the Gentile also. The rage of the townspeople stems from the centuries-old belief that they were God's special people. In their minds, the Gentiles are outsiders and cursed because they do not keep the law.

An insightful explanation for Jesus' miraculous escape may be found in Lot's rescue in Genesis 19:10–11. The angels struck the men of Sodom with blindness to protect Lot. Likewise, the men of Nazareth may have been blinded to allow Jesus to walk through their midst undetected. This blindness could manifest in other ways than the typical sense. It could extend to general perception such that the crowd simply did not notice where He was.

Some humorous modern-day phrases allude to this scripture, such as "dashing ahead where angels fear to tread" and "driving faster than angels can fly." These secular jokes imply that, due to our reckless behavior, the "left behind" angels are not there to catch us when we fall flat on our faces or crash, as the case may be (e.g., "lift you up lest you dash your foot against a stone!"—Psalm 91:12).

As holy beings, angels do the will of God. Since God cannot condone or facilitate sin, angels cannot support you in your efforts or intent to commit sinful acts. Their purpose is to protect, not enable sin. Jesus' promise in John 14:13–14 states,

> Whatever you ask in my name, this I will do, that the Father may be glorified in the Son.

This promise is followed by the condition stated in the next verse:

> If you love me, you will keep my commandments. (John 14:15)

In the case of the temptation of Jesus, Satan's purpose was to promote presumption. This is interesting because pride seems to be the sin that condemned Satan in the beginning.

Lesson

Although the promises of God are sure and true and we are to trust them in faith, it is quite another matter to be presumptuous and test Him through prideful or haughty behavior. Many who have thought they can follow a godless, pleasure-filled life and repent before they die are sadly mistaken when they die suddenly in a hit and run, struck by a stray bullet, or suffering an aneurysm.

Questions for Pondering

How well do I know the promises of God?

Have I acted presumptuously on the promises of God, many of which are conditional?

When is the last time I reread the promises for myself?

Chapter 13

Deserted!

In the above story, Jesus tells Satan, "Begone" (Matthew 4:10) and quotes Deuteronomy 6:13. Satan departs from Jesus, but have you noticed that he leaves Jesus stranded on top of the high mountain? It is here that we see the provision of Psalm 91:11–12 initiated! In Matthew 4:10 we are told that not only does Satan leave but angels come and minister to Jesus. This "ministering," in all likelihood, not only took the form of transporting Jesus back to where He needed to be but likely provided Him with food since the phrase implies more than an act.

Lesson

The promises of God are sure and true, and we are to trust them in faith. His provision in demonstrating His faithfulness sometimes take unexpected turns. The text does not specify how soon the angels came to minister, but it was likely very soon. At first glance, after Satan's departure, Jesus would have realized His predicament of being stranded. What do you bet that Jesus asked the Father for help and the angels were sent?

Questions for Pondering

Have I ever noticed that obedience to the Lord has left me in uncomfortable circumstances at times?

At such times, do I take my needs to the Lord?

If so, what happened? Thank Him for it.

Chapter 14

Acceptability of Cain and Abel's Respective Offerings

The story of Cain and Abel in Genesis 4 starts with the account of both men bringing an offering to the LORD, but while Abel's offering is acceptable, Cain's is not. Scripture states that Cain brought an offering of produce that was not accepted, but Able brought an animal sacrifice that was accepted. Many scholars deduce that since the ground was cursed, Cain's offering was cursed. There is a fallacy in this line of thought since some Levitical sacrifices included grain offerings that would also be cursed if this reasoning were valid. Later in scripture we discover that the covenant was based upon blood sacrifice; since Cain's offering is not blood based, this is the reason for its rejection. There seems to be something lacking in this explanation.

At the Fall, God delivers the curses to Satan, Adam, and Eve. The good news is the covenantal promise of Genesis 3:15. The story concludes with God making clothes for the couple and then expelling them from the garden. Several scholars have noted that the clothes God provided were made from animal skins, which implies the shedding of blood. The fact that blood was shed, though implied, could be a hint that this was an ancient remnant of a blood-covenant event.

Although no scripture had yet been written, the principles of the law are rooted in God himself. Looking ahead in scripture, one clear principle is that the righteous shall live by faith (Romans 1:17). A second principle is that of transference. The righteousness of God would be mine, and my sin would be transferred to Jesus to bear on the cross (2 Corinthians 5:21). Finally, without the shedding of blood, there is no forgiveness of sins (Hebrews 9:22).

The Genesis text says that Abel *also* brought (in addition to the grain offering or fruit of the ground) a lamb offering. That suggests that Abel brought this blood sacrifice to reconcile for sin prior to the votive or fellowship offering. Cain only brought a free-will offering without an attendant sacrifice for sin. The reason for Cain's sacrifice's being rejected becomes clearer when we read what God said to him in Genesis 4:7.

> If you do well, will you not be accepted? And if you
> do not do well, sin is crouching at the door. Its desire
> is contrary to you, but you must rule over it.

The issue is sin, but God addresses the issue cryptically. The subject first addressed is Cain's actions:

> If you do well (what is acceptable) then won't you be
> accepted? If you fail to do what is acceptable the sin is
> like an animal crouching before you.

The next sentence is puzzling, but the subject is implied in the Hebrew. Translators add the subject *sin* in most texts, but sin is neuter and not capable of "desire." Could it be possible that *sin* is not the subject but rather *Satan*? If this is so, the second half of this verse makes more sense. We know we are helpless to rule over sin, but through Christ we can and do rule (have authority over) Satan. One cannot prove this is the meaning of the text, but it is an interesting point to ponder.

Regarding sacrifices themselves, the text is silent, but one wonders if Adam offered sacrifices. And if he knew the need for blood sacrifice, did he teach it too or perform it before his children? Where did the idea to bring a sacrifice originate in the first place? How else did Abel know to bring the fat portions or specifically first fruits? It is noteworthy that Cain's sacrifice entailed only the cost of the produce and the labor he expended to tend it, while Abel paid the same price but in addition had an emotional price to pay in killing a heart-warming lamb.

Blood sacrifice is an ugly affair reminding the worshiper of the terrible penalty for sin. It is a stark reminder that, but for the grace of God, such would be my fate. When God gave Moses this story, the above details would have been included, considering the Levitical sacrificial system. The story is so ancient that the details of this story as well as the rest of the Genesis stories were likely narrated to Moses by God on Mt. Sinai in terms the people of Israel would understand. If God did not dictate these detailed events, then Moses must have used either oral history or ancient texts—or a combination thereof—preserved from the early forefathers.

Lesson

The penalty for sin is terrible and costly, but Jesus paid the price for me. When Jesus instituted the Lord's Supper, He said to do it in remembrance of Him. The major first step of this remembrance should be recalling the price He paid. The second step should be the celebratory joy we have remembering we are forgiven and will be with Him in heaven.

Question for Pondering

When was the last time I considered the cost of my sin?

When was the last time I joyfully "celebrated" the Lord's Supper as was the custom of the early church?[7]

Chapter 15

Joab Blood Vengeance Murder of Abner

The story of Joab's murder of Abner seems difficult to understand and discern the scriptural lesson. As is often the case, there is more to the story than what meets the eye. The story begins where there is war between Judah (David's tribe) and Israel (2 Samuel 2:19). Israel has been defeated by Judah, and Abner, the general of Israel, is fleeing, pursued by Asahel (brother of Joab and Abishai), one of David's mighty men (2 Samuel 2:19ff). Abner urges Asahel to stop pursuing him, but he refuses to turn aside. Therefore, Abner as he flees, strikes Asahel in the stomach with the butt of his spear, killing him. As the armies once again form opposite each other, Abner speaks to Joab and Abishai, asking them to stop pursuing their brothers Israel "lest war consume them." They heed Abner's plea, and the two armies go their separate ways. Abner (Saul's uncle) then installs Saul's son, Ish-bosheth, as king.

Later, Ish-bosheth insults Abner by accusing him of having relations with one of King Saul's concubines, which implies a ploy for the right to the throne. Insulted, Abner swears to "accomplish for David what the LORD had sworn to him," referring to David's anointing to be king of the entire nation in 1 Samuel 16.

The story continues in 2 Samuel 3:23–27:

> When Joab and all the army that was with him came, it was told Joab, "Abner the son of Ner came to the king, and he has let him go, and he has gone in peace." Then Joab went to the king and said, "What have you done? Behold, Abner came to you. Why is it that you have sent him away, so that he is gone? You know that Abner the son of Ner came to deceive you and to know your going out and your coming in, and to know all that you are doing." When Joab came out from David's presence, he sent messengers after Abner, and they brought him back from the cistern of Sirah. But David did not know about it. And when Abner returned to Hebron, Joab took him aside into the midst of the gate to speak with him privately, and there he struck him in the stomach, so that he died, for the blood of Asahel his brother.

David was extremely grieved over Abner's death. Several details need to be reviewed to understand the magnitude of this event. First, Joab was David's nephew, the son of his sister Zeruiah (1 Chronicles 2:16), and likely younger than David since David was the youngest of eight children.

Second, Joab and Abishai, his brother, killed Abner in blood vengeance because he had killed their brother Asahel in the battle at Gibeon. But Hebron was a city of refuge from the blood avenger. Legally, therefore, Joab and Abishai should have been executed for their murder of Abner at the gate of Hebron. David mourns Abner's death. The Masoretic Hebrew text says David curses Joab and his father's house (thus including Abishai in the curse) but only has Joab do penance (see 2 Samuel 3:30). However, the Dead Sea Scrolls give a variant translation: "May the blood of Abner son of Ner fall on Joab's head and on all Joab's house" (4QSam – the scroll of Samuel, found in cave 4 at Qumron).

Lesson

This is a long and complicated story with many details. It is easy to simply read the story, glossing over the many details, but with some detective work, the details allow for several fresh insights. Many nuggets of insight may be discovered by paying attention to details such as location, time, and relationships.

Question for Pondering

What details in my favorite Bible stories might enrich my Bible studies?

Chapter 16

Consequences: David's Regret

Have you ever wondered what the consequences were for allowing Joab and Abishai to live after the murder of Abner? Scripture declares Joab and Abishai to be among the best of David's thirty mighty men (2 Samuel 23:8ff). They were with David during the years King Saul was pursuing him. This loyalty coupled with being David's nephews (1 Chronicles 2:16) might explain David's hesitancy to execute them for murder.

David suffered several consequences for not executing Joab. The first was Joab's part in the plot to kill Uriah, Bathsheba's husband (2 Samuel 11:14–17). What is so ugly in this crime is David's betrayal. He writes orders for Joab to arrange for Uriah to be killed in battle and even has Uriah carry these "execution" orders to Joab! To make matters worse, Uriah was also one of David's thirty mighty men. This likely means Joab would have known him relatively well, if not intimately, from having likely fought side by side. So loyal Uriah is betrayed by both his king and his commanding general.

Second, when Absalom murders Amnon for raping his sister (2 Samuel 13:28) and flees to Talmai, king of Geshur, who is his grandfather (2 Samuel 3:3), Joab is instrumental in convincing David to reconcile with Absalom. But David fails to completely reconcile and thus lays the groundwork for Absalom to lead a revolt against King David, his father (2 Samuel 15). The next thing we discover is that Joab kills Absalom, his own cousin! This is in direct violation of David's express command (2 Samuel 18:5) to deal kindly concerning him. Then Joab rebukes David in his grief over Absalom's death (2 Samuel 19:4–8).

Joab is fickle and ambitious. David comes to his senses and reconciles and reunites the nation once again under his rule. In the process, Amasa (Joab's second cousin—2 Samuel 17:25), formerly a general of Absalom's army (2 Samuel 17:25), is made a general in Joab's place. This may have been David's response to punish Joab for killing Absalom. Later, Sheba heads another revolt, and David sends Amasa to organize the army but delays in following his orders. Joab takes matters into his own hands and kills Amasa (2 Samuel 20:5, 9–10). He assumes leadership as general of the army and puts down the revolt. This then makes Joab the de facto leader of the army again.

Now, fast-forward to the end of David's life. Joab supports Adonijah's bid to be king, forcing David to take drastic action in officially crowning Solomon as the new king. This seems to be the last straw for David as he finally gives Solomon orders to have Joab executed after David's own death (1 Kings 2:5). David was a slow learner, and Solomon did not need this bad man around to haunt his reign.

Not much is said about Abishai regarding his part in killing Abner. Scripture does recount his killing Goliath's brother, Ishbi-benob, who was attempting to take blood vengeance against David for killing Goliath (2 Samuel 21:16). In saving David's life in this way, Abishai may have been granted mercy and not executed at David's death. It may be that the Dead Sea Scroll variant indicates Abishai was only marginally involved in Abner's death despite the 2 Samuel 3:30 report that both men killed Abner. Another possibility is that Abishai may have already been dead by this time.

Lesson

This tragic story in David's life underscores the consequences of living in one's own wisdom. Family relationships notwithstanding, seeking God's wisdom on how to handle situations and doing what God requires is always the best course of action.

Questions for Pondering

Is it my practice to slow down before making any decision in my life and seek God's wisdom?

Do I search for wisdom in scripture?

Do I seek godly counsel as declared in Proverbs 11:14?

Chapter 17
Gaza's Gates Story: Revenge

The Old Testament contains many odd little stories, one of which is Sampson's carrying Gaza's city gates to the hill opposite Hebron. If you consider the details of this story, it becomes even more amazing. Here is the setting: Sampson is spending the night in Gaza, a Philistine city. The city officials become aware that he is there, and they lay a trap with armed guards at the city gates to capture and kill him. He gets up at midnight; rips the city gates, crossbar, posts, and all out of the wall; and carries them to the hill across from Hebron. It seems to be a simple enough story but think about it. Ripping the gates out of the wall must have been noisy and alerted the guards to Sampson's presence. So why did not the guards attack him? The text does not say. Perhaps Sampson got up before the guards were stationed.

Second, the gates themselves, if they are anything like the gates that are mounted on the Damascus gate in old Jerusalem today, would be extraordinarily heavy, approximately the weight of a small car. The two Damascus gates are made of solid wood and are about four inches thick, each approximately fifteen feet wide and maybe fifteen feet tall. Each is clad with bronze plates.

In addition to the weight, we have the fact that they would be unwieldy. Something similar would be carrying a half-inch-thick sheet of four-feet-by-eight-feet plywood any distance with even the slightest breeze. But Sampson carries the gates, together with the crossbar and posts, to the hill across from Hebron. This is a Jewish city approximately twenty miles from Gaza! Assuming he was walking on level ground (which he was not), *unencumbered* he could leisurely walk three to four miles per hour. With these assumptions it would have taken Sampson about five hours to walk that distance. In reality (barring supernatural speed), it would have likely taken longer. Since he got up at midnight, he would have then deposited the gates on the hill sometime around dawn, or later if he stopped to rest.

The key to understanding this story is to remember that Sampson's life is all about revenge. These Philistines are going to try to kill him, so he takes vengeance on them by stealing their city gates. The city gates are the prime means of defending a walled city, and as you might imagine they are not quickly repaired or rebuilt.

Sampson is in effect telling the Jews in Hebron that Gaza, an enemy Philistine city, is defenseless and they ought to attack before Gaza can rebuild the gates. Scripture is silent on whether they did, as well as on what happened at the gate with the guards. When one considers these details, the story becomes even more amazing!

Lesson

It is clear that God reserves revenge for Himself. The author of Hebrews writes in 10:30:

> For we know him who said, "Vengeance is mine; I will repay." And again, "The LORD will judge his people."

This is a quote from Deuteronomy 32:35–36. Yet it appears that Sampson was a tool for judgment (Judges 14:4). Although we cannot condone Sampson's actions, we can all agree he was badly abused by these ungodly people.

Questions for Pondering

Have I encountered a situation when I was tempted to seek revenge and did not do so but relied on God to vindicate me? It is some consolation that the book of Revelation details the horror of God's vengeance on apostate humankind.

Do I trust God enough to forgive and for vindication rather than revenge?

Chapter 18

Supernatural Deliverance of David from Saul

After David had killed the giant Goliath (1 Samuel 17:57), Saul was to give him his daughter in marriage as a reward (1 Samuel 17:25). Saul promotes David (1 Samuel 18:5) and offers Michal to David as his wife. But David is humble and hesitates because he is from a poor family and has no reputation (1 Samuel 18:23). Saul (who has become jealous of David) hatches a scheme to get rid of him, counters David's argument in verse 25, saying he will let David earn the dowry, or bride price, by providing the foreskins of a hundred Philistines — and in doing so be avenged of the king's enemies. Saul thought David would be killed trying to complete this task, but David successfully provides the bride price, frustrating Saul enough that he finally orders David to be killed. David is warned and flees to Ramah, Samuel's residence. Not to be outdone, Saul sends three groups of messengers to Ramah with orders to capture David (1 Samuel 19:18–24).

Saul is determined to kill David (1 Samuel 19:15), but God miraculously intervenes and causes His spirit to fall on each group Saul sends, at which point they fall helpless and start prophesying. In frustrated determination, Saul goes in person to do the job himself, but the spirit falls on him as well while he is on his way, and he begins prophesying too! Still determined, he continues and arrives at Naioth, where Samuel is. God intervenes more strongly and has Saul strip off his clothes and lie naked, prophesying all that day and night. The text of 1 Samuel 19:24 says, "And he too stripped off his clothes," which implies that this happened to the messengers as well. What is the significance of this incident?

On the surface it appears that God is simply protecting David. Yet other instances also involve the removal of clothes. Both Moses and Joshua were commanded to remove their sandals because these righteous men were standing on holy ground (i.e., in the presence of God). In this instance we have unrighteous men remove not only their sandals but also their clothes.

Additionally, the text does not record that this was holy ground, and nothing is said of others removing any clothing. The question is why would God lead them to remove their clothes when any number of other options were available? One possible explanation is that, for a king or a priest, clothes were a symbol of the authority and rank. By stripping off his clothes and possibly his weapons, Saul (as well as the evil spirit who tormented him) were stripped of all rank, authority, and power, left utterly defenseless. This lasted all day and all night, indicating that his rank and authority are his at the pleasure of the LORD. David used this time to escape from Saul.

We see in the next chapter that Saul has not learned his lesson or changed his mind. The demonic spirit tormenting him may have been behind his obsession to kill David since doing so would have ended the Messianic line. In 1 Samuel 20:33ff, Saul, in his anger, even tried to spear Jonathan, his son, during a religious feast for befriending David.

Lesson

God's provision takes many forms, from the mundane to the surprising. David, by staying with the prophet Samuel, is living out the example to which Jesus referred:

> If you abide in me, and my words abide in you, ask whatever you wish, and it will be done for you. (John 15:7)

> As the Father has loved me, so have I loved you. Abide in my love. (John 15:9)

Questions for Pondering

In thinking back, have I seen anything extraordinary happen in my life?

Can I see that these are indications of God's love for me?

Chapter 19

Greater Miracles than Jesus'

Truly, truly, I say to you, whoever believes in me will also do the works that I do; and greater works than these will he do, because I am going to the Father. (John 14:12)

The interpretation of just what the greater miracles are, has been one of the more difficult issues to understand. The traditional interpretation is that we do more miracles in number because there are more believers than the one Jesus. This sounds okay, but could it be that Jesus had something more in mind? In thinking about what Jesus said, what scale does one use to define *greater*?

In the attempt to see just what Jesus had in mind, we may wonder what greater miracles might look like. In the investigation of this idea, there seems to be an alternative interpretation of Jesus' statement. Could it possibly be that the miracles would be different and more amazing in character?

The search for an answer started by looking for any unusual

circumstance found in the Old Testament stories. Were there any miracles or attempted miracles that might have a counterpart in the events recorded after Pentecost? The surprise came in the discovery of an instance where Elisha attempted to resurrect a dead child and failed.

> He said to Gehazi, "Tie up your garment and take my staff in your hand and go. If you meet anyone, do not greet him, and if anyone greets you, do not reply. And lay my staff on the face of the child." Then the mother of the child said, "As the LORD lives and as you yourself live, I will not leave you." So, he arose and followed her. Gehazi went on ahead and laid the staff on the face of the child, but there was no sound or sign of life. Therefore, he returned to meet him and told him, "The child has not awakened." (2 Kings 4:29–31)

Then the realization hit that it is never recorded that Jesus ever attempted anything like this; He either spoke or laid hands on people, and they were healed or raised from the dead. Then the reason for the event concerning the apostle Paul in Acts 19:11–12 became obvious:

> And God was doing *extraordinary* miracles by the hands of Paul, so even handkerchiefs or aprons that had touched his skin were carried away to the sick, and their diseases left them and the evil spirits came out of them. (emphasis added)

Paul, it seems, would send sweaty handkerchiefs (literally) or aprons that he had touched to the sick or possessed, and they would recover or be delivered. This seems to be an example of Jesus' promise being fulfilled.

Likewise, when Peter's shadow fell on people in the street, it would cause them to recover or be delivered.

> And more than ever believers were added to the Lord, multitudes of both men and women, so that they even carried out the sick into the streets and laid them on cots and mats, that as Peter came by at least his shadow might fall on some of them. The people also gathered from the towns around Jerusalem, bringing the sick and those afflicted with unclean spirits, and they were all healed. (Acts 5:14–16)

This passage does not say they were healed or delivered by Peter's shadow, but the implication is there. It seems that after Pentecost, in accordance with Jesus' words, the Holy Spirit manifested His power in new and amazing ways.

In a manner of speaking, the anointing of the Holy Spirit manifested in Paul's sweat or filled the shadow cast by Peter with healing light. Scripture uses both water (sweat in this case?) and light (shadow?) as symbols of the Holy Spirit. These two instances are recorded in Scripture, but one must consider that, through the centuries, many similar remarkable events occurred that were nothing like what is recorded being done by Jesus.

Lesson

Since we are in relationship with Jesus, we should expect the miraculous in our lives. Jesus' statement was a statement of fact.

Questions for Pondering

Since I know Jesus Christ and the Holy Spirit personally, how am I participating in the work of God?

What are the greater possibilities that God could do through me such that miracles would take place in my life?

Do I have eyes to see the opportunities to step out and be used for the miraculous?

Chapter 20

Wiser than Solomon

Here is a logic problem: Who in the Bible (apart from Jesus and God) is wiser than or has greater discernment than Jedidiah? Now you might quickly answer "Solomon," but that is a wrong answer!

How can that be, given that Scripture is clear in saying Solomon was the wisest of all men?

> Behold, I now do according to your word. Behold, I give you a wise and discerning mind, *so that none like you has been before you and none like you shall arise after you.* (1 Kings 3:12, emphasis added)

> And God gave Solomon wisdom and understanding beyond measure, and breadth of mind like the sand on the seashore. (1 Kings 4:29–31)

Need a hint? Keep reading.

Wiser than Solomon: Hint 1

The correct answer to the first question is "no one." Now comes the hard part: determining why that is the correct answer. The reason is more subtle than "because God said so." In today's culture, we have become used to the quick answer due to our short attention span (e.g., twenty-second TV commercials). The point of this riddle is to test your critical thinking skills. Can you think this through logically and not give up? If you are having a difficult time, I will give you a significant hint, but do not get discouraged. I have known several Bible scholars to struggle with this, and some have given up so that I had to give the explanation.

You have what it takes to figure it out.

Persevere!

You *can* do it!

Wiser than Solomon: Hint 2

> Then David comforted his wife, Bathsheba, and went in to her and lay with her, and she bore a son, and he called his name Solomon. And the LORD loved him and sent a message by Nathan the prophet. So, he called his name Jedidiah, because of the LORD. (2 Samuel 12:24–25)

Jedidiah means "beloved of the LORD." *David* means "beloved."

Lesson

Here is another example of paying attention to minor details found in related events in scripture.

Question for Pondering

Am I willing to carefully look at my next scripture reading and find a detail to see what I can discover that is not obvious?

Solomon Riddle Answer

The correct answer is no one because Jedediah and Solomon are one and the same person and you cannot be wiser than yourself!

Chapter 21

Elijah Fed by Ravens

And the word of the LORD came to him: "Depart from here and turn eastward and hide yourself by the brook Cherith, which is east of the Jordan. You shall drink from the brook, and I have commanded the ravens to feed you there." (1 Kings 17:2–4)

As you may know, ravens are scavengers and carrion-eating birds; therefore, they are unclean according to the Levitical law. Out in the American West in campgrounds, ravens and crows are called camp robbers because they come in and steal any food left out. Four things are of note:

1. Ravens were considered unclean, Elijah could not eat any food that they brought. But in this instance, since God gave specific direction it was okay.

2. The food—both the meat and the bread—was provided by God. It therefore would have been clean food and not carrion or scraps dropped on the ground inadvertently, as might have been the case if it had been stolen from a camp. It is

interesting that the text does not say whether the meat was raw or cooked, nor does it say where the ravens found the food. Bread, by its very nature, is a prepared food. It is not found naturally but is processed grain that is baked.

Additionally, it is contrary to God's nature to have the ravens steal the bread, so the food must have been supernaturally provided to the birds as was the manna provided to the children of Israel in the wilderness. How interesting that the theme of God's provision in the wilderness crops up again!

By implication, the ravens themselves must have been sanctified to be clean since to eat food that had touched anything unclean was then also considered unclean:

> Flesh that touches any unclean thing shall not be eaten. It shall be burned up with fire. (Leviticus 7:19)

3. Two scriptures come to mind regarding this story. The first is Peter's vision of the sheet full of unclean animals before he was to visit Cornelius, in Acts 10:10–20. In this instance Peter is prophetically told in a vision not to consider Gentiles unclean, that the gospel of the kingdom is for all peoples. The second scripture is found in 1 Timothy 4:4–5:

> For everything created by God is good, and nothing is to be rejected if it is received with thanksgiving, for it is made holy by the word of God and prayer.

Here Paul reminds Timothy that all food is clean if blessed by the Lord. This was important because of the "food offered to idols" controversy addressed in 1 Corinthians 8.

4. Since both meat and bread were provided, it is interesting to note that Elijah did not have to live on bread alone, as Jesus told Satan, quoting Deuteronomy 8:3.

Lesson

Elijah still suffered through the drought and was in hiding. God was aware of his difficulties and, at the right time, brought him relief. The relief came in the form of sending him into the wilderness with special provision.

Questions for Pondering

Am I going through a hard time of suffering or in a wilderness?

Jesus reminded His disciples that they are of more value than many sparrows; in these situations, am I reminding myself of God's promises in scripture?

What does Matthew 28:20 mean — "And behold, I am with you always, to the end of the age"?

How is having Jesus at my side a comfort?

Jesus sent the comforter (Holy Spirit), so how is He comforting me during trials?

Do I see the ways?

Chapter 22

Sling and Staff: Weapons against Goliath

Almost every time I hear someone relate the story of David and Goliath, the emphasis is that David fought Goliath with a sling. What is interesting is that David went down to meet Goliath with not only a sling but also his staff. The text of 1 Samuel 17:40 states:

> Then *he took his staff in his hand* and chose five smooth stones from the brook and put them in his shepherd's pouch. His sling was in his hand, and he approached the Philistine. (emphasis added.)

In the story, Goliath's first words upon seeing David are,

> And the Philistine said to David, "Am I a dog, that you come to me with sticks?" And the Philistine cursed David by his gods. (1 Samuel 17:43)

All that Goliath sees at a distance from behind his shield is David's staff, totally overlooking the sling in his other hand. David exhibits great confidence in God, as indicated by his response. Verse 49 says,

> And David put his hand in his bag and took out a
> stone and slung it.

To do this, he needed two hands so either he laid down his staff (maybe), or he stood still, leaned the staff against his shoulder, and loaded the sling. Now if you have ever watched someone sling a stone, you quickly realized that doing so does not require two hands, nor do you need to whirl the stone around your head repeatedly before releasing it. Sometimes it is slung with one smooth motion—underhand, side arm, or over your head, as it is traditionally shown.

Second, it is not necessary that the events happened in exactly the order they are presented since David ran toward his enemy. It is possible that some of the events happened concurrently or in altered order since running with a staff and loading the sling seem mutually exclusive. The writer made a choice to tell the events in a certain order.

Going back to the issue of David's staff, we are reminded of David's Twenty-Third Psalm. We have no record of when David wrote this psalm, but since it is a shepherd's psalm, odds favor it being written before this battle. Here is why. Let's look specifically at verse 4:

> Even though I walk through the valley of the shadow
> of death, I will fear no evil, for you are with me; your
> rod and your staff, they comfort me.

In this story, Goliath is the valley of the shadow of death incarnate!

A sheep of a fold will see the shepherd with his ever-present staff and may get touched by it as the shepherd provides guidance or correction. The touch brings comfort in a similar way touching a dog during training will bring the dog's mind and attention to the present task and away from a distraction. This is like the staff in David's hand or leaning against his shoulder; it gave him the comforting reminder of God's presence and protection.

Lesson

David was a man of passion and walked in relationship with God. Granted, he walked in confidence, having God's promise to be the next anointed king of Israel. Mistakes notwithstanding, he was a man of the Word. The staff was the tool of the shepherd, a practical reminder of his Abrahamic covenant, and a comfort.

Questions for Pondering

What provides me comfort—a place, comfort food, people?

Does your Bible provide you comfort?

If not, what will it take to make it a source of comfort?

Would memorizing promises from God's Word help?

Chapter 23

The Helper (Parakletos)

Jesus told the disciples in John 14:16 that He would ask the Father to send another (*allos*) helper. There are two Greek words for "another"—one is of the same kind (*allos*), and the other is of a different kind (*heteros*; see John 19:37). The one used here is another of the *same* kind, implying that Jesus is also a helper. The word for *helper* in Greek is *parakletos*, which is also translated as "intercessor," "counselor," "advocate," and "comforter." Much has been said about the role of the Holy Spirit regarding the definition of *helper*.

Now let us look at this idea through the lens of friendship with the Trinity. Jesus comforted his disciples by assuring them that he would be with them even unto the end of the age, Matthew 28:20. He also sits at the right hand of the Father interceding for the saints which as we see in the above definition puts Jesus in the role of "helper."

What about the Father as a helper or comforter? The very idea of fatherhood opens a whole new line of thought. In a normal family situation, a young child can be comforted in several ways.

One is that the parent can speak comforting words.

But the Helper, the Holy Spirit, whom the Father will send in my name, he shall teach you all things, and bring to your remembrance, all that I have said unto you. (John 14:26)

Second, the parent can reach down and take the child's hand, as in Matthew 14:31 (Peter walking on water), and Mark 8:23 (leading the blind man). Finally, the parent could pick up and carry the child. This imagery is informed by the following verse:

Give, and it will be given to you. Good measure, pressed down, shaken together, running over, will be put into your lap. For with the measure you use it will be measured back to you. (Luke 6:38)

The English word *lap* is the translation of the Greek word *kolpos,* (Strong's Lexicon #G2859), "the front of the body between the arms, the bosom of a garment, or the hollow formed by the upper forepart of a rather loose garment bound by a girdle or sash used for keeping and carrying things." A similar idea is conveyed by bosom:

He will tend his flock like a shepherd; he will gather the lambs in his arms; he will carry them in his bosom (Strong's Lexicon #H2436), and gently lead those that are with young. (Isaiah 40:11 parenthetical note added)

You yourselves have seen what I did to the Egyptians, and how I bore you on eagle's wings and brought you to myself. (Exodus 19:4)

These scriptures recall the poem entitled "Footprints in the Sand,"[8] a fitting sentiment reflecting the comforting role of Father friend!

Lesson

Paul understood this principle quite well.

> No temptation has overtaken you that is not common
> to man. God is faithful, and he will not let you be
> tempted beyond your ability, but with the temptation
> he will also provide the way of escape, that you may
> be able to endure it. (1 Corinthians 10:13)

Questions for Pondering

Have I availed myself of any of these avenues of escape:

- Focus on worship and praise until the temptation passes?
- Spend time in prayer for my concerns and those of the kingdom?
- Read the word for encouragement regarding this situation, focusing on His promises?
- Contact a fellow believer with whom I can share and pray?

Chapter 24

Doing What He Saw the Father Do

A common misconception is that Jesus did *and said* only what He saw and heard from the Father. This idea is derived from John 5:19 and John 12:49–50, where Jesus said that he received a commandment from the Father and said what he was told by the Father. The Father's desire is to give eternal life, but this should not be interpreted to say that everything that Jesus said was an instruction from the Father. If so, how could he pray on His own behalf in John 17 or in Gethsemane at the start of his passion?

> So, Jesus said to them, "Truly, truly, I say to you, the Son can do nothing of his own accord, but only what he sees the Father doing. For whatever the Father does, that the Son does likewise." (John 5:19)

> For I have not spoken on my own authority; but the Father who sent me, has Himself given me a commandment, what to say, and what to speak. And

I know that his commandment is eternal life: what to
say and what to speak. (John 12:49–50)

I have read these passages dozens of times, but until recently I
had never considered the implications. I looked at the miracles Jesus
performed and could immediately see most of their counterparts
in the Old Testament stories. But then I came to some of the more
surprising miracles, such as changing water into wine and walking
on water, and the counterpart miracle in the Old Testament was not
so apparent. Following are some of the more obscure ones:

- Walking on water: In Matthew 14:25, Jesus has sent the
  disciples on ahead to cross the Sea of Galilee, and later during
  the night he walks on the water out to the boat. In the Old
  Testament, Elisha helps one of the prophets who lost an axe
  head in the river while cutting some timber. Elisha throws a
  stick into the water, and the ax head floats (2 Kings 6:1–7).

- Changing water to wine: In John 2:3–10, Jesus and some of
  His disciples are celebrating at a wedding in the town of Cana
  not too far from His hometown of Nazareth. During the
  usual weeklong celebration, the family runs out of wine. Jesus
  intervenes and instructs the servants to fill water jars with
  about thirty gallons of water and take some out for the maître
  d'. He pronounces that this is superb wine, not knowing it
  was formerly water. (Note that this being an exceptionally
  large quantity of wine; not all of it would be consumed, so
  the excess could have been sold with the proceeds going to
  bless the newlyweds.)

This miracle of transmutation has two counterparts: one in 2 Kings 2:19–22, where Elisha purifies bad water, and the second in 2 Kings 4:39–41, where he makes poison stew edible.

In the first, Elisha uses salt to purify the bad water in Jericho, and in the second he makes the poisoned stew edible with flour. Salt and flour are both elements used in covenant ceremonies. Salt is a purifying and preserving element (representing the eternal nature of covenant); thus, "the water is pure to this day." And flour is the primary element of unleavened bread, which is only flour and water. Jesus' body is the provision for our healing (Isaiah 53:5). In the wedding at Cana, Jesus assists in the celebration of the covenant of marriage.

- Feeding the five and four thousand: These miracles are described in Matthew 14:19–21 and 15:36–38. The Old Testament account is found in 2 Kings 4:42–44, where twenty loaves of barley and fresh ears of grain in one man's sack feed a hundred men with some to spare.

- Cursing the fig tree during Passion Week: With New Testament accounts in Mark 11:12–14 and 20–21, this miracle stems from the curse uttered by Jotham against Abimelech, his brother and the son of Gideon, after he murdered seventy of his brothers. Abimelech was unfaithful to his call and thus judged. And God also made all the evil of the men of Shechem return on their heads, and upon them came the curse of Jotham, the son of Jerubbaal. (Judges 9:57)

Another example is Elisha pronouncing a covenantal curse on the young men who were mocking his fresh anointing via Elijah.

He went up from there to Bethel, and while he was going up on the way, some small boys[9] came out of the city and jeered at him, saying, "Go up, you baldhead! Go up, you baldhead!" And he turned around, and when he saw them, he cursed them in the name of the LORD. And two she-bears came out of the woods and tore forty-two of the boys. (2 Kings 2:23–24)

Elijah's response to their jeering stems from the command found in Exodus 22:28:

You shall not revile God, nor curse a ruler (leader) of your people (parenthesis added).

And 1 Samuel 26:9 adds:

But David said to Abishai, "Do not destroy him, for who can put out his hand against the LORD's anointed and be guiltless?"

In like manner the fig tree failed to produce fruit, which was symbolic of the Jewish leaders who were coming against Jesus—God's anointed.

- Peter's temple tax (Matthew 17:24ff) being supernaturally provided by a fish through Jesus' direction: This word-of-knowledge miracle probably is related to Elisha's being able to warn King Ahab of pending attacks against Israel by the king of Syria (2 Kings 6:12) and Elijah being fed by the ravens in 1 Kings 17:2–6. Additionally, it may be linked to the provision of the ram for sacrifice in place of Isaac on Mount Moriah, since

Abraham said the LORD would provide the sacrificial animal. The ram had to start his journey up the mountain to get caught in the thicket prior to Abraham's building the altar!

- Peter's great catch of fish (Luke 5:4ff): This miracle is covered by authority over nature and animals as in the plagues of Egypt or through a word of knowledge as shown in the provision of quail in the desert (Exodus 16:13).

- Delivering from demonic oppression or possession (Luke 8:27–38): The man from whom the demons had gone begged that he might stay with Jesus, but He sent him away, saying, "Return to your home, and declare how much God has done for you." And he went away, proclaiming throughout the whole city how much Jesus had done for him.

There is no direct Old Testament story directly relating to deliverance from demonic influence except what is implied in the case of Saul. In 1 Samuel 17:14–16, we are told that Saul has an evil spirit (demon?), and David was tasked to play a lyre to bring him relief. The story continues with a deep sleep from the LORD overcoming Saul and his army in 1 Samuel 26:12–14. By inference, the deep sleep from the LORD may have been a deliverance. This may be similar to the deliverance of Mark 9:26 where the boy is left like a corpse. Saul responds to David's rebuke with repentance and in his right mind, as did the freed demoniac in the New Testament story. Jesus implies as much in Luke 11:20:

> But if it is by the finger of God that I cast out demons,
> then the kingdom of God has come upon you.

Lesson

Jesus promised his disciples that when the Holy Spirit came, they would do greater miracles than He. In my own strength I can do nothing, but

> I can do all things through Him[10] who strengthens me. (Philippians 4:13)

Question for Pondering

As I walk in obedience to Jesus, getting to know His character, do I have the boldness and confidence to do what He would do or asks— big or small?

Chapter 25

Sampson's Nazirite Vow Violations

The Nazirite vow, as described in Numbers 6:1–8, was a voluntary heart attitude vow. When one took a Nazirite vow, they were required to never to cut their hair for the duration of the vow and forbidden to drink alcohol, eat grape products, or touch a dead body, neither human nor animal. In this story (Judges 14:6–9), Sampson is going to Timnah with his parents to get a Philistine bride. On the way, a young, roaring lion comes toward him, and he kills the lion when the Spirit of the LORD comes upon him (Judges 14:6–9). Later, Sampson finds a beehive in the carcass and scrapes out some of the honey. Because the honey is from a dead carcass, it is unclean (i.e., not kosher). He gives some of the honey to his parents but does not tell them where he got it. They would have known that it was unclean and would not have eaten it. Normally, this would have been a violation of his Nazirite vow, meaning the time he had spent under the vow would be negated and must be restarted by shaving his head and making sacrifices. But in Sampson's case, he had not make the vow voluntarily. Sampson's Nazirite status was imposed from before his birth, so his heart was not engaged in being voluntarily dedicated to God but for revenge on the Philistines.

> His father and mother did not know that it was from the LORD, for he was seeking an opportunity against the Philistines. At that time the Philistines ruled over Israel. (Judges 14:4)

This made his Nazirite status a special case in that it was not negated in touching a dead body. If this was not the case, he would have also violated his Nazirite status when he killed a Philistine. To underscore this, Judges 14:19 and 15:14–15 say that the Spirit of God came upon him, enabling him to slaughter the Philistines. God's purpose in all this was to fulfill a curse against the Philistines, according to Genesis 12:3:

> I will bless those who bless you, and him who dishonors you I will curse, and in you all the families of the earth shall be blessed.

Lesson

We have something similar to Sampson's situation today in the form of infant dedication and baptism. Apart from the theological implications associated with these, there seems to be a pattern evident in these children's lives. It seems as if the hand of the Lord is upon these children and circumstances seem to favor their making commitments for personal relationships with Jesus Christ as their savior. Granted, the indicators may be skewed due to the influence and prayers of their parents and sponsors, but one must wonder.

Questions for Pondering

Have I thought about what God's purpose is for my life?

Have I become aware of any area where God has provided unusual success in my work or activities?

Chapter 26

All Things New

Revelation 21:1 and 4ff states that John saw a new heaven and earth, then the one "who was seated on the throne said, 'Behold, I am making all things new.'"

In the Greek text, the literal translation is "I am making all new." What is of note is that God calls attention to the fact that He is *presently making,* not that He will make or has made. In the first verse, John sees the newly created heaven and earth, so this cannot be what God is talking about! If the new heaven and earth are excluded (since they are already made), what then is left to be made new?

Two things come to mind. The first is relationships.

- Interpersonal: perfect fellowship with saints and with God seeing Him in His unrestrained glory.

   For where two or three are gathered in my name,
   there am I among them. (Matthew 18:20)

- No marriage: Jesus explained to the Sadducees that the redeemed in heaven would not marry (Luke 20:34–36,

Matthew 22:29–30). We would like to know more details about this marriage statement. If there is no marriage, then does it follow that there will be no need for sex and therefore childbirth? We are never told in Scripture that angels have children. That stems from popular myth.

The second deals with how we will spend our time.

- Nature: There will no more curses on the ground or us, no weeds to toil over, and no pain in childbirth (Genesis 3:16–17).
- Children: We will no longer need to procreate (Genesis 1:28, 9:1).
- Possibly new types of work and mission: With all men and women in perfect relationship with God, there will no longer be a need to go and make disciples (Matthew 28:19–20).

Lesson

It appears our future life in heaven will be anything but boring. What do ruling and reigning with Jesus look like (2 Timothy 2:11)? This "living with Him" will come with a whole new way of being; all the old ways will have passed away.

Question for Pondering

How could my trials and life lessons be preparing me for what lies ahead in heaven?

Chapter 27

Guards at the Tomb on Resurrection Day

When we retell the resurrection story on Easter, we already know it tells of guards at the tomb to prevent anyone from stealing Jesus' body. We get excited about the angel rolling the stone aside and his announcement of "He is risen." But all too often we overlook the details regarding the guards. Matthew 28:2–8 shares the detail that they are what some in the charismatic movement call "slain in the Spirit."

It is easy to overlook that the guards were present when the angel spoke to the women and that this interchange is what some of them reported to the chief priests. Note that the text does not say that the women obeyed the angel and looked inside the tomb. When the women were on the way to tell the disciples, Jesus met them. The guards would not have witnessed this interchange or the later appearance to Mary after John and Peter left the tomb.

Another detail is that only some of the guards went to report to the chief priests (Matthew 28:11). These were the ones paid to spread the lies concerning Jesus' body being stolen. One wonders about the other guards. Seeing a lightning-bright-white-clad angel could only be reported by an eyewitness. I suspect that the ones who did not go would have told the truth at some point or became believers themselves. The Pharisees were the ones who set the guard and sealed the tomb, not Pilate. It follows that these were temple guards, not Roman soldiers. If they were Roman soldiers, they would have been executed. Since they were temple guards, they would report to the chief priests not to Pilate.

One additional detail often overlooked is that the women were worried about who would roll back the stone (Mark 16:2–4). It is apparent that they were unaware that the tomb had been sealed and guards were stationed to prevent the stone from being moved and the body stolen. It is amusing to ponder how these guards and what additional army could prevent the one angel from moving the stone!

Lesson

When there are parallel accounts of the same story, it is helpful to compare the details and how they complement and support each other.

Questions for Pondering

In situations where I have seen the Lord work, what has been the reaction of the bystanders?

- Is there skepticism, or has it given them pause to reflect?
- In these situations, am I willing to boast in the Lord?

> But let him who boasts boast in this, that he understands and knows me, that I am the LORD who practices steadfast love, justice, and righteousness in the earth. For in these things I delight, declares the LORD. (Jeremiah 9:24)

- Use this space to record events you or someone you know has experienced; that have been miraculous or extraordinarily coincidental.
- In looking back, can you see God's hand at work?

Chapter 28

Early Church Relationships

For most of us, family relationships are difficult at times and impossible at others. As followers of Jesus, family relationships can be even more strained because of the disparity between worldly and godly values. The interpersonal relationships detailed in the Gospel accounts bring into focus the reality that Jesus' ministry did not happen in a vacuum but involved real people. By detailing the family relationships and the life problems they entail, we are connected since we face these same issues to varying degrees. This is another detail that helps us take our family concerns to Jesus since He understands the issues we face.

> Therefore he had to be made like his brothers in every respect, so that he might become a merciful and faithful high priest in the service of God, to make propitiation for the sins of the people. For because he himself has suffered when tempted, he is able to help those who are being tempted. (Hebrews 2:17–18)

> For we do not have a high priest who is unable to sympathize with our weaknesses, but one who in

every respect has been tempted as we are, yet without sin. Let us then with confidence draw near to the throne of grace, that we may receive mercy and find grace to help in time of need. (Hebrews 4:15–16)

So just what were some of the relationships referenced in the Gospel accounts? In the following examples, each person is given a superscript number for tracking. Let us look at some of the details at the crucifixion.

Standing by the cross of Jesus were his mother[1] and his mother's sister,[2] Mary the wife of Clopas,[3] and Mary Magdalene.[4] (John 19:25)

There were also many women there, looking on from a distance, who had followed Jesus from Galilee, ministering to him, among whom were Mary Magdalene[4] and Mary the mother of James and Joseph[5] and the mother of the sons of Zebedee.[6 or 2] (Matthew 27:55–56)

There were also women looking on from a distance, among whom were Mary Magdalene,[4] and Mary the mother of James the younger and of Joses,[5] and Salome.[7, 6 or 2] (Mark 15:40)

Matthew reports that there were many women standing at a distance, identifying a few important ones. Mark reports only three notable names. Why is Salome one of the notables mentioned here by name?

By checking the superscripts for each name, Salome is possibly Jesus' aunt (His mother's sister); the mother of James and John; the wife of Zebedee; or another unknown woman. If she is an unknown woman who was simply at the crucifixion scene, why would she show up in Mark's list in the first place? It follows she must have had some significance to be mentioned by name. Could it be that Salome is the same person in these three gospel accounts? If she is Mary's sister, then James and John were Jesus' cousins. If this is the case, we see both acceptance and rejection among members of Jesus' family. The cousins reacted favorably and followed Jesus, but the siblings and even His mother at one time sought to interrupt or direct His ministry:

> Then he went home, and the crowd gathered again, so that they could not even eat. And when his family heard it, they went out to seize him, for they were saying, "He is out of his mind." (Mark 3:20–21)

> And his mother and his brothers came, and standing outside they sent to him and called him. And a crowd was sitting around him, and they said to him, "Your mother and your brothers are outside, seeking you." (Mark 3:31ff)

> After this Jesus went about in Galilee. He would not go about in Judea, because the Jews were seeking to kill him. Now the Jews' Feast of Booths was at hand. So his brothers said to him, "Leave here and go to Judea that your disciples also may see the works you are doing. For no one works in secret if he seeks to be known openly. If you do these things, show yourself to the world." For not even his brothers believed in him. (John 7:1–5)

They thought Him out of His mind or at least naive, since they, like everyone else, thought the Messiah was to be a political deliverer; so, they were seeking to rouse public support. It is not clear why His mother was asking for Him but noteworthy that it was probably His whole family, including James, who later became a prominent leader in the early church.

Lesson

Setting aside the speculation of Salome being His aunt, family and friends sought to influence Jesus to modify His earthly mission. We are to continue to pray and persevere for our family members even though we may not see much progress. We may not see any change in their decisions to follow Jesus or attempts to dissuade us from doing so. Living our relationship with the Savior speaks much louder than any words we may use to preach to the unsaved in our sphere of influence. Living a godly life and honoring the Lord in all we do has an impact on those we live among. In the end, Jesus persuaded His brother James to the point that James became the leader of the early church in Jerusalem. This is not to say we don't need to be ready to explain why we live and believe as we do.

> But in your hearts honor Christ the Lord as holy, always being prepared to make a defense to anyone who asks you for a reason for the hope that is in you; yet do it with gentleness and respect, having a good conscience, so that, when you are slandered, those who revile your good behavior in Christ may be put to shame. (1 Peter 3:15ff)

Questions for Pondering

How can my attitude show my love toward those in my family or sphere of influence?

How do my attitudes and conversations reflect on the Savior?

When family or friends trigger my emotions, do I then let my emotions cause me to react badly? Do not let guilt or condemnation cause me to question the promises and truths found in God's Word?

In my interactions, do I consider the answer to the question, "What would Jesus do?"

Chapter 29

Why Pray Twice to Heal?

> And he took the blind man by the hand and led him out of the village, and when he had spit on his eyes and laid his hands on him, he asked him, "Do you see anything?" And he looked up and said, "I see people, but they look like trees, walking." Then Jesus laid his hands on his eyes again; and he opened his eyes, his sight was restored, and he saw everything clearly. (Mark 8:23–25)

Supernatural healing continues to be a controversial issue. The above instance where Jesus prays twice for the blind man to be healed is sometimes used to explain why someone receiving healing requires multiple prayers. The explanation is "Even Jesus needed to pray twice!" However, this statement poses a theological problem. Did Jesus, who knows the perfect will of God, have a failure in this prayer—namely, an incomplete healing? This contradicts the teaching of Jesus' own words:

> The Father loves the Son and has given all things into his hand. (John 3:35)

And Jesus came and said to them, "All authority in heaven and on earth has been given to me." (Matthew 28:18)

So Jesus said to them, "Truly, truly, I say to you, the Son can do nothing of his own accord, but only what he sees the Father doing. For whatever the Father does, that the Son does likewise." (John 5:19)

It follows that if Jesus performed an incomplete healing the first time He prayed, then He did not have all authority or was not doing what the Father was doing. Therefore, Jesus must have been intentional in this two-step healing. In the passages immediately preceding this instance, Jesus rebukes the disciples for their lack of perception following the feeding of the four thousand in the beginning of chapter 8:

And they began discussing with one another the fact that they had no bread. And Jesus, aware of this, said to them, "Why are you discussing the fact that you have no bread? Do you not yet *perceive or understand*? Are your hearts hardened? Having eyes do you not see, and having ears do you not hear? And do you not remember?" (Mark 8:16–18, emphasis added)

Healing someone's eyesight is not only a physical event but a spiritual one as well. Elisha prayed that his servant's spiritual eyes be opened and later prayed for an army to be struck blind and later healed (2 Kings 6:15–18).

Either John 3:35 is wrong, or more likely the healing process was intentional. If intentionality is the case, then there is a purpose here, for Jesus never did anything by accident. Therefore, Jesus must be teaching something here. The key to this is found in John 9:39–41:

> Jesus said, "For judgment I came into this world, that those who do not see may see, and those who see may become blind." Some of the Pharisees near him heard these things, and said to him, "Are we also blind?" Jesus said to them, "If you were blind, you would have no guilt; but now that you say, 'We see,' your guilt remains."

The key to interpreting this teaching lies in what the blind man first saw, men walking as trees. Scripture records many instances of men compared to trees. The most familiar quote is found in Psalm 1:1–3:

> Blessed is the man who walks not in the counsel of the wicked, nor stands in the way of sinners, nor sits in the seat of scoffers; but his delight is in the law of the LORD, and on his law he meditates day and night. He is like a tree planted by streams of water that yields its fruit in its season, and its leaf does not wither. In all that he does, he prospers.

Lesson

Divine healing is a complicated and controversial topic. The reasons for some being healed and others not ultimately lies with God's sovereignty. Asking why is the wrong approach in this regard. Below are three more pertinent questions.

Questions for Pondering

How is my attitude in times of trouble, suffering, or sickness?

Am I prepared to accept the answer to the questions,

1. What are you doing?
2. How am I to participate? and
3. What am I to learn?

Chapter 30

Wisdom of Birds

And Elihu answered and said … who teaches us more than the beasts of the earth and makes us wiser than the birds of the heavens? (Job 35:1, 11)

Of the four friends who came to speak to Job, Elihu was the only one not chastised by the LORD.

After the LORD had spoken these words to Job, the LORD said to Eliphaz the Temanite: "My anger burns against you and against your two friends, for you have not spoken of me what is right, as my servant Job has. Now therefore take seven bulls and seven rams and go to my servant Job and offer up a burnt offering for yourselves. And my servant Job shall pray for you, for I will accept his prayer not to deal with you according to your folly. For you have not spoken of me what is right, as my servant Job has." So Eliphaz the Temanite and Bildad the Shuhite and Zophar the Naamathite went and did what the LORD had told them, and the Lord accepted Job's prayer. (Job 42:7–9)

With this in mind, we can take Elihu's statements as trustworthy. So, for example, just what is the wisdom of birds exactly? If we do a thorough study of bird behavior, it becomes apparent there are two categories of behavior. The first is what is called instinct, such as flying south for the winter in the northern hemisphere. There is no wisdom in such behavior that Job or we could readily benefit from. What remains is survival behavior. Birds generally are very aware of their surroundings. They are constantly on the lookout for predators. Their general defense is to fly away, but this is less effective against birds of prey. Some birds will escape to the branches of a tree rather than take to the sky.

What is the wisdom lesson for us? The Bible speaks to this issue in 1 Peter 5:6–8:

> Humble yourselves, therefore, under the mighty hand of God so that at the proper time he may exalt you, casting all your anxieties on him, because he cares for you. Be sober-minded; be watchful. Your adversary the devil prowls around like a roaring lion, seeking someone to devour.

As birds remain mindfully aware of their environment, we need to do likewise. We must rely on the Lord's care and protection, even as the birds rely on God's provision as Jesus pointed out in Matthew 6:26:

> Look at the birds of the air: they neither sow nor reap nor gather into barns, and yet your heavenly Father feeds them. Are you not of more value than they?

Lesson

Applying the wisdom of birds, we too must be ever mindful of the spiritual battle while we go about our daily tasks. The words in 1 Peter 5:8 — "Be sober-minded; be watchful"—relate directly to the wisdom of the birds. Being sober-minded is being discreet or sober; the word *watchful* is a different Greek word meaning to keep awake or vigilant. It is so easy to fall prey to the old adage "out of sight, out of mind."

Questions for Pondering

What action can I take to increase my awareness of my spiritual enemy's efforts to bring me harm?

What are the ways available to me to take advantage of the provision and protection provided by the Father, as Peter said?

Chapter 31

Jesus the Intercessor

My little children, I am writing these things to you so that you may not sin. But if anyone does sin, we have an advocate with the Father, Jesus Christ the righteous. (1 John 2:1)

Consequently, he is able to save to the uttermost those who draw near to God through him, since he always lives to make intercession for them. (Hebrews 7:25)

The English word *intercede* is from a Latin word of two parts: *inter* meaning "between" and *cedere* meaning "go." An intercessor is a go-between. Jesus stands between us and the Father; by His presence, He stands as our personal advocate, wordlessly pleading our case.

Jesus does not need to continually remind or intercede to the Father on our behalf for salvation, as if the Father could ever forget the fact. His very presence and His scars do that, so just what is the nature of His interceding?

When we are in the midst of trials or suffering in one form or another, it is common to experience the "tides of faith." The imagery is startling and informative. When the ocean tide is low, the scenery of a bay is stark and uninviting, and it stinks. At times such as these, we are tempted to doubt, asking,

- Did God hear my prayer?
- Why don't I see an answer?
- Is Jesus still interceding for me?

When the tide is coming in, reminders come flooding in with it. People often cross our paths, giving word of reminders or encouragement, such as

- What then shall we say to these things? If God is for us, who can be against us? (Romans 8:31)
- Jesus Christ is the same yesterday and today and forever. (Hebrews 13:8)
- I am praying for them. I am not praying for the world but for those whom you have given me, for they are yours. All mine are yours, and yours are mine, and I am glorified in them. (John 17:9–10)
- I do not ask that you take them out of the world, but that you keep them from the evil one. (John 17:15)
- I do not ask for these only, but also for those who will believe in me through their word. (John 17:20)

At high tide, many things are covered and the landscape is quite different. This is a time of miraculous faith! But no matter the time, the water of faith may still be seen. One aspect of Jesus' intercession is seen where, prior to the crucifixion, Jesus encourages Peter.

Simon, Simon, behold, Satan demanded to have you, that he might sift you like wheat, but I have prayed for you that your faith may not fail. And when you have turned again, strengthen your brothers. (Luke 22:31–32)

But there is another aspect of intercession: He intercedes on behalf of the church, His body, and His bride. The Old Testament relates the ongoing concern for the Jewish nation from whom the Messiah was to come. It is apparent that God was answering the prayers of His people. God answers before we even ask.

Before they call, I will answer; while they are yet speaking, I will hear. (Isaiah 65:24)

A glaring example is the story of Daniel's fasting and prayer. In Daniel 9, intercession is made by Daniel on behalf of his people.

Then I turned my face to the LORD God, seeking him by prayer and pleas for mercy with fasting and sackcloth and ashes. I prayed to the LORD my God and made confession, saying, "O LORD, the great and awesome God, who keeps covenant and steadfast love with those who love him and keep his commandments, we have sinned and done wrong and acted wickedly and rebelled, turning aside from your commandments and rules. … O LORD, hear; O LORD, forgive. O LORD, pay attention and act. Delay not, for your own sake, O my God, because your city and your people are called by your name." (Daniel 9:3–5, 19)

As we read on, Daniel discovers his prayer was answered right away, but there was spiritual resistance for him to get the answer.

> Then he said to me, "Fear not, Daniel, for from the first day that you set your heart to understand and humbled yourself before your God, your words have been heard, and I have come because of your words. The prince of the kingdom of Persia withstood me twenty-one days, but Michael, one of the chief princes, came to help me, for I was left there with the kings of Persia, and came to make you understand what is to happen to your people in the latter days. For the vision is for days yet to come." (Daniel 10:12–14)

So the archangel Michael was dispatched to aid Gabriel in delivering the answer. Jesus is proclaimed to be the same yesterday and today and forever in Hebrews 13:8. Jesus stated in the garden of Gethsemane that the Father would dispatch angelic help if Jesus asked (Matthew 26:53). It follows that His intercessory role may be at work here too as He directed angelic aid in this spiritual battle.

Lesson

The pattern is revealed: we have an enemy who resists our prayers, but Jesus commanded us to pray to the Father in the name of Jesus (John 16:23ff). There is a caveat for this statement, and it presupposes an abiding in Jesus. Having a vibrant relationship with Him and the Father results in knowing His character and heart. Then we can ask, knowing with certainty it is His will.

Questions for Pondering

What ways have I found to abide in and with Jesus?

How about praying for Him to reveal new ways to enrich my abiding?

Chapter 32

Who Told You Were Naked?

Have you ever thought about the question God asks Adam and Eve: "Who told you you were naked?" (Genesis 3:7–11). This question seems to be out of place. It suggests that somehow they were actually *not* naked. But Genesis 2:25 says,

> And the man and his wife were both naked and were
> not ashamed.

In our way of thinking, they were naked in that they had no clothes. What in effect may have happened is that God pointed out that there was a change in their spiritual status. They reacted to their change of status by making fig-leaf clothing, trying to compensate for their spiritual change. Yet in reality, they were clothed spiritually in filthy rags, which replaced their garments of holiness.

It is very clear from Scripture that we will be clothed in robes of righteousness:

> I will greatly rejoice in the LORD; my soul shall exult
> in my God, for he has clothed me with the garments

of salvation; he has covered me with the robe of righteousness, as a bridegroom decks himself like a priest with a beautiful headdress, and as a bride adorns herself with her jewels. (Isaiah 61:10)

It is also likely that this robe is white (in Israel, white symbolized royalty) and holy because it has been washed in the blood of Jesus.

I said to him, "Sir, you know." And he said to me, "These are the ones coming out of the great tribulation. They have washed their robes and made them white in the blood of the Lamb." (Revelation 7:14)

Note that Jesus was buried naked, simply wrapped in linen cloths that were, by the way, left inside the tomb at the resurrection. Yet no one considers Him naked in His appearances to the women or disciples. One must conclude He was indeed wearing clothes, as we will in our resurrected bodies.

These robes may be new.

Then they were each given a white robe and told to rest a little longer, until the number of their fellow servants and their brothers should be complete, who were to be killed as they themselves had been. (Revelation 6:11)

Lesson

Being clothed in Jesus' robe of righteousness is not only a positional state but appears to also be a physical one as well. But it is not yet seen with our natural eyes. St. Patrick had the right idea:

Christ with me, Christ before me,
Christ behind me, Christ in me,
Christ beneath me, Christ above me,
Christ on my right, Christ on my left,
Christ when I lie down, Christ when I sit down,
Christ when I arise.

Questions for Pondering

Like St. Patrick, am I presence obsessed?

How might my day be affected if I, as I get dressed, consciously put on a garment of praise for the day?

Chapter 33

Eve as Helpmate

The story of the origin of humankind has been the subject of much discussion through the centuries, as has the subject of Eve being Adam's helpmate. The observation that she was formed from Adam's rib indicates that she is equal and a joint heir; she was not made from his feet so he could walk over her nor from his head indicating her dominance (Genesis 2:22ff). In the secular culture, the role of women has been demeaned, curtailed, and in some cases severely distained and limited. Historically, in Judaism and even more so in Christianity, women have been given esteem and recognition of their worth. Despite the great advancements for women in education, society, and the workplace, there is yet one aspect that has been sorely overlooked.

This deficiency has to do with the word *helper* referenced in Genesis 2:18:

> Then the LORD God said, "It is not good that the man
> should be alone; I will make him a helper fit for him."

The Hebrew word for *helper* means "help," "succor," or "one who helps." This same word is used in some psalms.

Behold, God is my helper; the LORD is the upholder of my life. (Psalm 54:4)

The LORD is on my side as my helper; I shall look in triumph on those who hate me. (Psalm 118:7)

In the New Testament, the Greek word bears a similar meaning.

But the Helper, the Holy Spirit, whom the Father will send in my name, he will teach you all things and bring to your remembrance all that I have said to you. (John 14:26)

The husband then has a wife who serves in many similar ways as the Holy Spirit—helper, counselor, intercessor, companion, and friend. Being intuitive, women often hear from the Spirit when men do not. Over the many centuries, male-driven societies have focused on women's gender roles, overlooking the great benefits delegated to the helpmate role. The spiritual sensitivity of a godly woman is a gold mine, making a chauvinistic husband vastly poorer for his failure to cherish his helpmate.

Lesson

Marriage is ultimately a partnership where gender defines certain roles. Wise is the husband who nurtures and encourages his wife to press into a deeper relationship with the Lord and seriously considers her spiritual insights. His role, likewise, is to seek to deepen his own relationship with the Lord in order to lead his family with wisdom, some of which will be derived from his helpmate's insights.

Questions for Pondering

Are there any areas in my life where pride has interfered with listening to or speaking into the life of my spouse?

Are there any areas in my life where I have failed to submit to the wisdom God has ordained in my marriage or how I relate to the opposite gender?

Wives, do you submit to the godly leadership of your husbands?

Husbands, do you lay down your wants in favor of meeting the needs of your wife?

Chapter 34

Oreo Cookie Offer

Do you remember the Oreo cookie jingle: "A kid'll eat the middle of an Oreo cookie first, leaving the chocolate cookie outside till last"? I was amused, and then I discovered the sobering "Oreo cookie" of Isaiah.

One day while musing through the Old Testament book of Isaiah, I noticed it had sixty-six chapters and for some reason was led to the first, middle, and last chapter of the book. Following is what I discovered.

The Oreo Cookie Outside: The Offer

> Come now, let us reason together, says the LORD: though your sins are like scarlet, they shall be as white as snow; though they are red like crimson, they shall become like wool. If you are willing and obedient, you shall eat the good of the land; but if you refuse and rebel, you shall be eaten by the sword; for the mouth of the LORD has spoken. (Isaiah 1:18–20)

I was meditating on the colors scarlet and crimson and noted the comparison, and the idea dawned on me that the color of sin is red.

The dye is even derived through death for it comes through crushing the dried body of a certain female insect (coccus ilicis). And the word *crimson* is compared to the word *adam,* meaning "red." This insect is referenced in a prophetic Messianic Psalm:

> But I am a worm and not a man, scorned by mankind and despised by the people. (Psalm 22:6)

The worm referenced here is the crimson tola grub. The following is quoted from DiscoverCreation.org[11]:

> The Hebrew word used here for worm, is TOLA'ATH, which means "Crimson worm" or "Scarlet worm." Both scarlet and crimson are the colors of blood—deep red. The Crimson worm [coccus ilicis] is a very special worm that looks more like a grub than a worm. When it is time for the female or mother Crimson worm to have babies (which she does only one time in her life), she finds the trunk of a tree, a wooden fencepost, or a stick. She then attaches her body to that wood and makes a hard crimson shell. She is so strongly and permanently stuck to the wood that the shell can never be removed without tearing her body completely apart and killing her.
>
> The Crimson worm then lays her eggs under her body and the protective shell. When the baby worms (or larvae) hatch, they stay under the shell. Not only does the mother's body give protection for her babies, but it also provides them with food—the babies feed on the LIVING body of the mother!

After just a few days, when the young worms grow to the point that they are able to take care of themselves, the mother dies. As the mother Crimson worm dies, she oozes a crimson or scarlet red dye which not only stains the wood she is attached to, but also her young children. They are colored scarlet red for the rest of their lives.

After three days, the dead mother Crimson worm's body loses its crimson color and turns into a white wax which falls to the ground like snow.

Following are some other interesting facts about the Crimson worm:

1. The crimson worm is common in the region of old Israel.
2. In ancient days the dead bodies of the female Crimson worms were scraped from the tree, dried, and then ground into a powder that was used to dye cloth and garments a scarlet or red color.
3. They are round and about the size of a pea. Because they don't look like a worm, some people have thought they were part of a plant.
4. The crushed worm was also used to make medicine that helps the heart beat smoothly.
5. The white wax body was used to make shellac, a preservative of wood.

The Oreo Cookie Filling: Accepting the Offer

Hear, you who are far off, what I have done; and you who are near, acknowledge my might. The sinners in Zion are afraid; trembling has seized the godless: "Who among us can dwell with the consuming fire? Who among us can dwell with everlasting burnings?" He who walks righteously and speaks uprightly, who despises the gain of oppressions, who shakes his hands, lest they hold a bribe, who stops his ears from hearing of bloodshed and shuts his eyes from looking on evil, he will dwell on the heights; his place of defense will be the fortresses of rocks; his bread will be given him; his water will be sure. (Isaiah 33:13–16)

Here we see the sweet benefits of accepting the offer of chapter 1, to dwell in God's presence with protection and provision. This is for those who have their sins covered by the blood of the Lamb!

The Oreo Cookie Outside: The Alternative—Rejecting the Offer

And they shall go out and look on the dead bodies of the men who have rebelled against me. For their worm (tola) shall not die, their fire shall not be quenched, and they shall be an abhorrence to all flesh. (Isaiah 66:24)

By not accepting the offer, one continues to be covered by the scarlet and crimson stain of sin.

Lesson

This is a vivid description of the fate of the lost at the last judgment. So the offer is before you—choose this day whom you will serve.

Question for Pondering

Have I procured the gift provided by Jesus' life, death, and resurrection walking with Him as a friend and no longer dependent on my own efforts to be good enough? If not, go back and read chapter 4.

Do I conduct periodic evaluations of my Christian walk? A good time would be prior to partaking the Lord's Supper.

- Examine if I am walking righteously and speaking uprightly?
- Do I seek justice, love mercy and am walking humbly with the Lord? (Micah 6:8)

Chapter 35

The Pain of Pruning

John 15 has been the subject of a great deal of study, and sometimes consternation, regarding the subject of pruning and abiding with Jesus.

> I am the true vine, and my Father is the vinedresser. Every branch in me that does not bear fruit he takes away, and every branch that does bear fruit he prunes, that it may bear more fruit. Already you are clean because of the word that I have spoken to you. Abide in me, and I in you. As the branch cannot bear fruit by itself, unless it abides in the vine, neither can you, unless you abide in me. I am the vine; you are the branches. Whoever abides in me and I in him, he it is that bears much fruit, for apart from me you can do nothing. (John 15:1–5)

Often when we make the comparison between humans and plants in this pruning analogy, we get caught up in the literalness and relate to the pain. Let's explore this assumption. The two terms of interest are *takes away* and *prune.* Jesus is talking about a vineyard and the vinedresser. Scientifically speaking, the grapevine and plants in general have no nerves and so cannot feel pain. The two Greek words describe two types of actions. The Greek word for *take away* generally means just that, but it also implies "lift up," which describes one task of a vinedresser.

When a branch lies on the ground and gets buried or covered by dirt, the vinedresser lifts and cleans off the branch and then ties it onto the trellis so it can be fully exposed to the sun. The branch then becomes healthy and productive. The second word is *prune,* which means cutting off unproductive branches. What is pruned takes the form of branches of three types: dead, sucker, or unproductive.

Obviously, a dead branch is unproductive, but it also could damage a healthy branch or the vine by causing it to break due to its weight or by harboring disease. A sucker will never produce fruit but draws away nutrients that would otherwise go to fruit-producing branches.

The last type is a branch that is unproductive due to location or disease. A branch may be growing in or toward a direction that will result, if unchecked or unguided, in unproductiveness or death.

Lesson

The pain of pruning is not necessarily a physical pain but is often associated with letting go of hopes or desires in order to follow the new direction revealed by the Lord. In a similar way, this is like the master carpenter showing his apprentice the correct way to use a tool or what tool to use for a specific task. By following the new direction, the apprentice is one step closer to mastering what is needed to produce the beautiful cabinet.

Questions for Pondering

Do I have an area where I am holding on to a want or dream, despite knowing the Lord is speaking to me to let go or go in a different direction?

Do I trust the Lord enough to allow Him to bless me in new ways by going in a different direction?

Chapter 36

Bestowing Value

Have you ever thought about how value is determined? For example, how about money (the dollar bill), gold, or property such as land, homes, or racehorses? In thinking about it, some things have intrinsic value, such as gold or cut gems. Other things have value because of what someone will give for it, such as money.

But what about the dollar bill? Why does it have value? The answer is simply that the government backs it with value. In reality, at face value it is only paper printed with colored ink. The German people found their money to be worthless prior to the Second World War during out-of-control inflation. Other methods of valuation are determined by what one can do or achieve with the item, such as a racehorse's potential for winning the Kentucky Derby. The famous racehorse Secretariat was worth over $16 million after winning the Triple Crown.

Other evaluations are less exact. For example, how do we value some costume jewelry? It may only be worth a few dollars, or the cost of the metal or glass that it is composed of. Yet if it belonged to your favorite grandmother, then it has sentimental value. Try as you might, you really cannot put a price on that! Generally speaking, something has value based upon what someone is willing to pay for it. As can be attested to by many, this value can change over time.

Now we come to a very important item for valuation: people. How does one determine the value of a person, or more specifically, how does one determine one's own value? Far too often, people have low-self-esteem because they have not forgiven themselves for some wrong they have done, actual or perceived. They may have hurt someone they care deeply for. Or worse still, they may believe lies they were told, saying that they are no good or will never amount to anything.

However, this is a false valuation. Value is determined by another method, a far more important one. This method is explained in the Bible.

> For God so loved the world, that he gave his only Son,
> that whoever believes in him should not perish but
> have eternal life. (John 3:16)

God the Father valued you so much that He sacrificed His son to pay the price to redeem you from death and restore you to an intimate relationship with Him. Further, Jesus Christ, the divine son of God, never changes in "value," as Hebrews 13:8 states: "Jesus Christ is the same yesterday and today and forever."

The value of the Son of God is infinite, so no higher price could be paid on your behalf—therefore giving you incredible and inestimable value.

Lesson

With this principle in mind, since we have been esteemed of such a high value by Father God, then when we value other people, they are likewise vested with value. He values all people, and when we do the same, this results in a tangible boost to their self-worth.

Question for Pondering

How can I show that I value those whom the Lord brings across my path?

Chapter 37

The Voice of God

> And after the wind an earthquake, but the LORD was not in the earthquake. And after the earthquake a fire, but the LORD was not in the fire. And after the fire the sound of a low whisper. (1 Kings 19:12)

Many people are troubled by the concept of the still, small voice talking to Elijah in the Old Testament. It might be better translated as "whisper." Regardless, the trouble stems from the question, "How do I know God is talking to me?" Much has been written on this subject, but often confusion results from the stereotypical image brought to mind above.

Judaism has a term for the divine voice, *bath kol*, that translates as "daughter of the voice" or "echo." If you ever listen to an echo, you quickly realize that the echo is not the same as the original sound but returns a little less distinct or not as crisp sounding. There are overtones in the sound due to multiple reflecting surfaces. In some cases, the echo is so garbled that you cannot distinguish what the original sound was. The reflected sounds overlap, with some time delay, causing the returning sound to interfere with the original. Scripture likens God's voice to that of thunder:

Have you an arm like God, and can you thunder with
a voice like his? (Job 40:9)

So why the use of the thunder symbolism? Apart from the awesomeness of God as the source, let us consider a thunderclap following a lightning bolt. The electric bolt of lightning tears through the atmosphere, leaving a vacuum in its wake. The thunder is the sound of the air retuning to fill the vacuum. The return of the air follows the path the bolt took, much the same way water flows in a stream or river when a dam breaks upstream. The wave races down the course of the channel, producing a racing, moving sound. Thunder is never a crisp sound but a confused cacophony.

Why then would the term *bath kol* or *echo* be used to describe God's voice? Why the idea of distortion or nonclarity? There must be some explanation for this sense of distortion since God does not make mistakes and obviously wants us to understand what He says. One explanation is that the voice of God speaks to our spirits.

God speaks to us in terms we can understand and can relate to, depending on our circumstances. In Elijah's case, we find a man suffering a great depression and panic. This followed a great spiritual victory, attended by a miracle over idolatry on Mount Carmel (1 Kings 18). So how do we get the attention of someone who is frightened and depressed? In Elijah's case, God enabled him to fast for forty days while he ran away from Jezebel, traveling about a hundred miles! When Elijah finally stopped to rest in a cave, the LORD showed up and broke up Elijah's pity party (1 Kings 19:9–10). Still not restored and brought to his senses, it took a mighty wind, an earthquake, a fire, and *then* a whisper to finally get his attention!

Elijah eventually got serious, but when one has a "stiff neck" or hardened heart or is controlled by fear, the message of the voice is unintelligible (thunder). Something similar occurred in 1 Samuel 7:10:

> As Samuel was offering up the burnt offering, the Philistines drew near to attack Israel. But the LORD thundered with a mighty sound that day against the Philistines and threw them into confusion, and they were defeated before Israel.

In this case, when Israel is in the midst of a revival, turning back to worship God, the Philistines, enemies of Israel, choose to attack. God speaks to them, but because of their idolatrous determination, they cannot understand the voice and are thrown into confusion. In this case, the Philistines are dead in their idolatry.

At other times it is possible that what was heard was directed only to an individual, so all others heard it as thunder.

> Now Mount Sinai was wrapped in smoke because the LORD had descended on it in fire. The smoke of it went up like the smoke of a kiln, and the whole mountain trembled greatly. And as the sound of the trumpet grew louder and louder, Moses spoke, and God answered him in thunder. (Exodus 19:19)

It is clear that thunder has a language since John was prohibited from writing down what he heard the thunders say.

> And when the seven thunders had sounded, I was about to write, but I heard a voice from heaven saying, "Seal up what the seven thunders have said, and do not write it down." (Revelation 10:4)

At other times one hears but, due to one's preconceptions, misinterprets what is spoken. In John 12:28ff, God spoke and the crowd was mixed about what they heard:

> "Father, glorify your name." Then a voice came from heaven: "I have glorified it, and I will glorify it again." The crowd that stood there and heard it said that it had thundered. Others said, "An angel has spoken to him."

Those who rejected Jesus and His words were dead in their sin of unbelief and could only hear thunder, but the ones who were sensitive to the spirit of what Jesus was teaching and had ears to hear were enabled to discern the words of the Father's response to Jesus' prayer request.

Lesson

For us, since God likely speaks Spirit to spirit, God's message may be as simple as a stray thought entering our minds or as complicated as a dream or vision. The task remains to consider the thought's source, to discern whether it stems from us, God, or Satan. The determining factor is whether the thought is in harmony with scripture, brings a sense of peace, reflects God's character, and is something outside of what we would normally think. At times, some have difficulty in testing the words against scripture. Either they do not know the Word (due to lack of study) or believe a distorted view, based on someone else's understanding of scripture (a "hear-say" gospel). In testing anything against scripture, whether teaching or prophesy, Proverbs 11:14 gives us a clue:

Where there is no guidance, a people falls, but in an abundance of counselors there is safety.

Seek counsel from trusted, mature believers for help in judging the word against scripture. In hearing prophesy, you must not get discouraged if you miss it, if the message is misheard or interpreted wrong. Keep listening. God is faithful! With practice you can learn to recognize the voice of God and gain confidence in sharing a prophetic word or acting on what you hear.

Question for Pondering

Do I have anyone who is mature with whom I can share what I hear for help and confirmation?

Chapter 38

Cattle Fodder

Have you ever wondered about Israel's flocks and herds during the forty-year sojourn in the wilderness? How could the wilderness support the vast number of livestock? The daily sacrifices required by the tabernacle worship needed significant numbers of sheep, goats, and cattle. If the estimate of two million people leaving Egypt with their livestock is accurate, then the livestock must also have numbered in the millions as well. Even if the semiarid land they were living in was lush green pasture at the time of the exodus, maintaining the livestock would have been a problem.

Recognizing the faithfulness of God and the provision and care He established for the forty-year sojourn in the wilderness, it seems inconsistent that He would not have provided for their livestock as well. It is noteworthy that no mention is made of this fact in scripture. So what was the provision made for the people? He provided water:

> When they came to Marah, they could not drink the water of Marah because it was bitter; therefore it was named Marah. And the people grumbled against

Moses, saying, "What shall we drink?" And he cried to the LORD, and the LORD showed him a log, and he threw it into the water, and the water became sweet. There the LORD made for them a statute and a rule, and there he tested them. (Exodus 15:23–25)

He also provided water from a rock in Exodus 17:6 and Numbers 20:8–11. And finally, Deuteronomy 8:3–4 adds,

And he humbled you and let you hunger and fed you with manna, which you did not know, nor did your fathers know, that he might make you know that man does not live by bread alone, but man lives by every word that comes from the mouth of the LORD. Your clothing did not wear out on you and your foot did not swell these forty years.

God saw to it that their clothes did not wear out, provided water out of the rock, and sweetened the bad water, but for food He provided manna. Pondering the question of how the livestock were fed, we must not rule out supernatural growth of grass or foliage for the livestock. However, due to the lack of any reference to that in scripture, this seems unlikely.

The only other obvious solution is the manna. It is highly possible that even as Israel gathered the daily manna, the livestock could have grazed on it as well. Being supernatural in nature, it must have had all the mineral, vitamin, protein, and trace elements required to maintain physical health. It would not be outside of God's provision to also provide the same nutrition for the livestock.

Lesson

In the prayer of Jabez, God answered his prayer. And in doing so Jabez would never know all the harm he was spared and the pain God had kept from Him.

> Jabez called upon the God of Israel, saying, "Oh that you would bless me and enlarge my border, and that your hand might be with me, and that you would keep me from harm so that it might not bring me pain!" And God granted what he asked. (1 Chronicles 4:10)

Questions for Pondering

Do I have eyes to see God's miraculous provision in my life?

Ask God to show you how He is involved in the mundane things in your life.

Chapter 39

A Heap of Crowns

> The twenty-four elders fall down before him who is seated on the throne and worship him who lives forever and ever. They cast their crowns before the throne. (Revelation 4:10)

This passage is intriguing in that it is not clear who these twenty-four elders are. The Greek word for *crown* is *stephanos,* from an apparently primary root *stepho* ("to twine or wreathe"); it is a *chaplet* (as a badge of royalty, a prize in the public games, or a symbol of honor, generally; but more conspicuous and elaborate than the simple *fillet).*

Additionally, it does not identify the type of crown. Several crown types are mentioned in scripture.

- Reward: Philippians 4:1, Paul refers to his converts as his crown (reward?)
- Righteousness: 2 Thessalonians 4:8
- Of life: James 1:12
- Of glory: 1 Peter 5:4
- Golden crown: Revelation 14:14, this verse may be referring to the glorified Savior

These crowns may all be referring to the same thing since Jesus, in His dictated letter to the angel of the church of Philadelphia, referred to their crowns in the singular (Revelation 3:11). The biblical example of what was done when going to a king or prophet was to bring a gift (see 1 Samuel 9:7).

Jesus referred to storing up treasures in heaven (Matthew 6:19–21). A crown represents a valuable treasure; if modeled after the European pattern, it was made of gold and encrusted with precious jewels. Assuming our treasure in heaven is or represents our crown, then we may very well follow the lead of the twenty-four elders and lay our crowns before King Jesus. If this is the case, then the millions upon millions of saints casting their crowns before the King of Kings would create a heap of crowns indeed!

Lesson

Whatever the nature of our treasure, all that we have will be gladly offered to the Lord in that day, following the example of the twenty-four elders.

Questions for Pondering

What is the nature of the treasure we are building in heaven?

What might constitute wood, hay, and stubble?

What might constitute gold, silver, and precious stone?

Use this space to record your thoughts answering these questions.

Chapter 40

Man Being Alone

Then the LORD God said, "It is not good that the man should be alone; I will make him a helper fit for him." (Genesis 2:18)

Have you ever wondered just what it was about being alone that was not good? God simply states the fact and proceeds to correct the problem by creating Eve. Considering Adam's situation, he had everything that was needed for his prosperity and general happiness. At that point, there was no sin or curse in the world. What God did to correct the deficiency was to create a new relationship and with it the human community.

When Jesus was asked what the greatest commandment was, He responded with two in Matthew 22:35–40:

And one of them, a lawyer, asked him a question to test him. "Teacher, which is the great commandment in the Law?" And he said to him, "You shall love the LORD your God with all your heart and with all your soul and with all your mind. This is the great and first commandment. And a second is like it: You shall love your neighbor as yourself. On these two commandments depend all the Law and the Prophets."

In the divine community of the Trinity, there is mutual perfect love. This horizontal component to the two great commandments could not be experienced by Adam.

He could only experience vertical fellowship (i.e., the first great commandment). Until Eve, there was no opportunity to experience the benefits of obeying the second great commandment.

From God's perspective, the second great commandment is being perfectly observed in the divine community. After the fall, God eventually gave the law at Mount Sinai. The commands were not needed by God but for the benefit of humankind. Being holy, the character of God has no flaws. He is therefore perfectly open-handed and generous (Psalm 145:15–16, 19–20).

Lesson

Although the second great commandment is probably the most difficult to fully obey, it is the one with the greatest near-term reward. The reward is seen in two ways:

- First, the principle of sowing and reaping dictates that we will be repaid by people in greater proportion than we sowed.

    Give, and it will be given to you. Good measure, pressed down, shaken together, running over, will

be put into your lap. For with the measure you use
it will be measured back to you. (Luke 6:38)

- The second benefit is in the formation of the mind and character of Jesus.

> But when one turns to the Lord, the veil is removed. Now the Lord is the Spirit, and where the Spirit of the Lord is, there is freedom. And we all, with unveiled face, beholding the glory of the Lord, are being transformed into the same image from one degree of glory to another. For this comes from the Lord who is the Spirit. (2 Corinthians 3:16–18)

When all is said and done, heaven is a community where everyone is most concerned about meeting the needs of every other person and every other person is most concerned about your needs.

Questions for Pondering

Apart from the short term, have I ever given or helped someone without eventually seeing a blessing from the Lord as a result?

If I have regrets in this regard, do I have eyes to see the blessings the Lord is pouring out on me, as promised in Luke 6:38?

Chapter 41

Crumbs in God's Economy

But she came and knelt before him, saying, "Lord, help me." And he answered, "It is not right to take the children's bread and throw it to the dogs." She said, "Yes, Lord, yet even the dogs eat the crumbs that fall from their masters' table." Then Jesus answered her, "O woman, great is your faith! Be it done for you as you desire." And her daughter was healed instantly. (Matthew 15:25–28)

Jesus seems harsh in His treatment of the Syrophoenician woman. It is important, however, to remember that Jesus is the promised Messiah to Israel regarding the Abrahamic covenant. Israel is designated as a nation of priests (Exodus 19:6–8). Remembering that the purpose of the priest was to function as an intermediary between people and God, the nation of Israel was to be the intermediary between God and the Gentile nations. Jesus' purpose was to enable Israel in their role as a nation of priests. This Gentile woman's faith in the sufficiency of a mere crumb in God's kingdom economy was the point of Jesus' comment and her reward.

Lesson

God's superabundance in His provision is always more than enough for our needs. The difference between a big and small miracle is the same difference one observes in the heights of Mount Everest and the Dead Sea when viewed from the moon. From God's viewpoint, there is nothing too difficult; His provision is always more than enough to meet our need.

Questions for Pondering

Do I tell God about my problems, or do I tell my problems about my God who loves and promises to care for me?

Chapter 42

Zeal of God

Zeal is defined as "eagerness and ardent interest in pursuit of something."[12] Consider how zeal relates metaphorically to the finger, hand, and arm.

The Finger

The finger is referenced in the Old Testament in three ways: creation (Psalm 8:3–4), the power of God (Exodus 8:18–19), and the giving of the law (Exodus 31:18). The psalmist states in metaphor that, by the work of the finger of God, the heavenly bodies were created. In the Exodus plagues, the Egyptian magicians attributed the creation of living lice in a plague to the finger of God. The last reference states that when God made an end of communing with Moses on Mount Sinai, the two tablets of stone were written with the finger of God.

In all three of these instances, the author uses metaphor. *Merriam-Webster's Collegiate Dictionary* defines *metaphor* as "a figure of speech in which a word or phrase, literally denoting one kind of object or idea, is used in place of another to suggest a likeness or analogy between them."

God, before the birth of Jesus, did not have a literal finger, yet, to convey a thought, a finger is ascribed to God as a word image. For us, as creatures of time and space, we can grasp the idea intended. We can envision a finger writing or doing the actions described. This is different from what King Belshazzer saw in the vision of the fingers of a hand writing on the wall (Daniel 5:5). Something tangible happened because physical writing appeared on the plaster for others to read and interpret.

Now let us look at a New Testament example. In Luke 11:19–20, Jesus asked the Pharisees,

> And if I cast out demons by Beelzebul, by whom do your sons cast them out? Therefore they will be your judges. But if it is by the finger of God that I cast out demons, then the kingdom of God has come upon you.

The finger metaphor is used to represent a certain level of involvement and authority—authority in that God got involved in the effort to create the universe, cast out demons, and give the Mosaic Law. In this involvement, even with zeal (that is eager desire or effort), using a finger, in physical terms, is less arduous than using a hand. In other words, I can do more with my hand than I can with only my finger.

The Hand

God so loved us, His creation, that He made this world for us to inhabit. The prophet Isaiah states,

> I made the earth and created man on it; it was my hands that stretched out the heavens, and I commanded all their host. (Isaiah 45:12)

This is how God showed his zeal. God, as the creator, is outside time and space. Therefore, as a spirit being, His actions cannot be adequately described to beings of time and space. A. W. Tozer, in addressing John 1:1, observes,

> A word is a medium by which thoughts are expressed, and in the application of the term to the eternal son, leads us to believe that self-expression is inherent in the Godhead, that God is forever seeking to speak himself out to his creation.[13]

God is an interactive God; something in His nature requires an ongoing relationship. Once again, the metaphor gives insight. Here the hand grasped and manipulated. In Genesis 2:7, 18, and 21–23, we see God getting involved with His creation. But God is not finished yet! Not only has He been involved, but He replicates aspects of himself in His creation of man. He has interacted with His creation on a personal level and now gives authority to His beloved creation (Genesis 1:26–27). In giving authority, dominion, and free will, He voluntarily limits Himself. The psalmist says it this way:

> You have given him dominion over the works of your hands; you have put all things under his feet. (Psalm 8:6)

He loves man so much that He transfers dominion and stewardship. Now we see a duality in operation here: since God is God, being the creator, all things belong to Him, yet He transfers authority and dominion. His involvement with us also is reflected by instilling in us a need to have fellowship with Him. We, as the created, recognize this and return to Him honor and gifts through worship.

King David made preparations to build a temple for worship and recognized God as the source, when he said,

> Both riches and honor come from you, and you rule over all. In your hand are power and might, and in your hand it is to make great and to give strength to all. (1 Chronicles 29:12–16)

The imagery of the potter and the clay from Isaiah 64:8 brings further insight. Making pottery is a very tactile art in which the potter skillfully uses his or her hands to repair and mold the clay. The process to prepare the clay for use is as follows: The first thing to be done is to select the proper proportions of clay, grout or sand, and water. These ingredients are mixed together, "wedged," and kneaded. This process is similar to kneading bread dough except that air is removed from instead of worked into the medium. If the air were not removed, the vessel would either become misshapen when being formed or crack or explode when fired in the kiln. Next, the clay is shaped by pressing and molding into the shape desired using both the fingers and hands. This process is done either by hand building or on a potter's wheel. After the vessel is formed, it is left to slowly air dry until relatively hard. At this stage, the vessel is called greenware. The greenware is fragile until it is fired in the kiln. The firing process drives out the excess water and causes the clay particles to fuse into stone. Some types of pottery can be glazed or decorated before firing; others are fired first, then glazed, and refired.

The symbolism for this example is very striking. Fire is a symbol for the Holy Spirit. The air pockets in the clay represent sin, which brings destruction if not removed. The molding process represents the tests and trials in life. The potter also puts part of himself or personality into his work, as he works and shapes the clay to give it character. When the potter does this, he puts love into his work and thereafter cares for his work and takes pride in it.

The Arm

A turning point in history brings the arm into play. The serpent in paradise causes the man and woman to become estranged in relationship through disobedience. This separation of humans from God requires God to intervene. Humankind is doomed for we cannot extract ourselves from the estrangement, so God does the "impossible"!

God's zeal for fellowship with us causes Him to initiate a plan of salvation. The metaphor reflects creation's reaction to His zeal.

> You with your arm redeemed your people, the children
> of Jacob and Joseph. Selah. When the waters saw you,
> O God, when the waters saw you, they were afraid;
> indeed, the deep trembled. (Psalm 77:15ff)

These passages are dealing with the rescue of Israel from slavery in Egypt, but just consider how the plagues reflect the fervor of God's zeal. Comparing the above salvation to what was required to accomplish the permanent salvation of the entire world, the cost of God's involvement is addressed in the fifty-third chapter of Isaiah. In this chapter we see the arm of the LORD revealed through the suffering of the Messiah.

Lesson

The progression of finger, creating the heavens; to hand, forming man; to arm, forging our salvation reflects the effort, cost, and magnitude of the zeal that God exhibited to restore humankind to fellowship with Himself.

Questions for Pondering

Analyze your current zeal.

Jesus charged the church at Ephesus with losing their first love (Revelation 2:1–8). Rewording that statement and applying it to myself, has my passion or zeal for Jesus cooled from the level observed when I first was saved?

How can I regain my former zeal?

If you are struggling to answer the above questions, ask the Holy Spirit for guidance or insight.

Chapter 43

Comforting an Angel

Then the angel of the LORD said, "O LORD of hosts, how long will you have no mercy on Jerusalem and the cities of Judah, against which you have been angry these seventy years?" And the LORD answered gracious and comforting words to the angel who talked with me. So the angel who talked with me said to me, "Cry out, Thus says the LORD of hosts: I am exceedingly jealous for Jerusalem and for Zion." (Zechariah 1:12–14)

From the context of this chapter, it appears that the Angel of the LORD in verse 12 is different from the "angel who talked with me" of verses 13 and 14. The text implies the presence of two angels since each angel is identified by location. Some scholars hold that the Angel of the LORD is a theophany or manifestation of God—namely, an appearance of the preincarnate Christ.

Earlier in verse 9, the "angel who talked with me" said, "I will show you what they are," and the other angel in verse 19 answered—that is, began speaking—which leads one to conclude that this is a different angel, although it is possible it is the same angel. If this is the same angel, why are the words *show* and *answered* used?

Either way it is to be understood, the LORD comforted the angel who was talking with Zechariah after the proclamation question in Zechariah 1:12. This statement presents a puzzle as to how to understand the situation.

1. The angel being comforted is the Angel of the LORD, the preincarnate Christ, which is supported by the statement that it was a man sitting on a red horse in the myrtle grove (verse 8). This poses a question: why would the Lord speak comforting words to the preincarnate Christ? Obviously, He needed emotional comfort, which is in keeping with what we understand of the human Christ Jesus.
2. The alternative understanding is that this was simply an angel who required emotional reassurance of some sort.

The conclusion is that angels (or at least one is) are capable of emotional responses. There is some indication that Gabriel was a bit annoyed at Zechariah for not believing his announcement of John's future birth through Elizabeth.

> And the angel answered him, "I am Gabriel. I stand in the presence of God, and I was sent to speak to you and to bring you this good news. And behold, you will be silent and unable to speak until the day that these things take place, because you did not believe my words, which will be fulfilled in their time." (Luke 1:19ff)

There may be other hints in scripture of angels exhibiting emotions, such as the angels who rescued Lot and his family. Lot lingers, and in exasperation the angels grab their hands, drag them out of the city, and then urge the four to flee. Lot, still stalling, commences to bargain:

> As morning dawned, the angels urged Lot, saying, "Up! Take your wife and your two daughters who are here, lest you be swept away in the punishment of the city." But he lingered. So the men seized him and his wife and his two daughters by the hand, the LORD being merciful to him, and they brought him out and set him outside the city. And as they brought them out, one said, "Escape for your life. Do not look back or stop anywhere in the valley. Escape to the hills, lest you be swept away." (Genesis 19:15–17)

Likewise, Satan, a fallen angel, has great wrath against the saints of God (Revelation 12:12).

Lesson

This puzzle may encourage us to reevaluate what we understand about angels. At the very least, angels may not be the emotionless automatons some consider them to be.

Questions for Pondering

In general, when evaluating a new or controversial subject, it is often helpful to ask oneself the following questions:

- How certain am I of the facts I hold as true?
- Am I aware of my presuppositions?
- How can I evaluate the presuppositions I hold as true?

Chapter 44

David's Unforgivable Sin?

Upon reading Psalm 51, there is a sense of not only desperate sorrow for sin but also despair. David states that he realizes that sacrifices and offerings will not atone for his sin or he would give them. This prompts a question: why are these insufficient? The answer to this question lies in the Levitical law. Some of the references are as follows:

- If one person sins *unintentionally*, he shall offer a female goat a year old for a sin offering. And the priest shall make atonement before the LORD for the person who makes a mistake, when he sins *unintentionally*, to make atonement for him, and he shall be forgiven. (Numbers 15:27–28, emphasis added)
- You rebuke the insolent, accursed ones, who wander (stray) from your commandments. (Psalm 119:21 parenthetical note added)
- The priest shall take some of the blood of the sin offering and put it on the doorposts of the temple, the four corners of the ledge of the altar, and the posts of the gate of the inner court. You shall do the same on the seventh day of the month for

anyone who has sinned through error or ignorance; so you shall make atonement for the temple. (Ezekiel 45:19ff)

These and many others make it clear that the Levitical sacrificial system was only for unintentional sins. There was no provision for a sacrifice to atone for an *intentional* sin. In King David's situation, it is obvious that he acted intentionally, breaking the law not only in committing adultery and betraying one of his mighty, loyal men but also in arranging his murder. In doing so, he also caused Joab to be complicit in the murder of Uriah. Consequently, David had no offering available for forgiveness.

As a result of his rebellious actions, David lived for nine months with his deception and the resultant guilty conscience and maybe awareness of the loss of fellowship with God. In Psalm 51:17, David reveals the key to his forgiveness, that it is a "broken spirit; a broken and contrite heart." God is interested in heart attitudes.

Jesus' sacrifice ended the ongoing need for sacrifices and gave provision for this kind of intentional sin. The author of Hebrews gives two main reasons why the New Covenant is better than the Levitical Covenant:

> But as it is, Christ has obtained a ministry that is as much more excellent than the old as the covenant he mediates is better, since it is enacted on better promises. For if that first covenant had been faultless, there would have been no occasion to look for a second. For he finds fault with them when he says: "Behold, the days are coming, declares the LORD, when I will establish a new covenant with the house of Israel and with the house of Judah, not like the covenant that I made with their fathers on the day when I took them

by the hand to bring them out of the land of Egypt. For they did not continue in my covenant, and so I showed no concern for them, declares the LORD. For this is the covenant that I will make with the house of Israel after those days, declares the LORD: *I will put my laws into their minds, and write them on their hearts,* and I will be their God, and they shall be my people. (Hebrews 8:6–10, emphasis added)

Here again the point is made that God is interested in the heart attitude.

Lesson

Under the mediation of the New Covenant by Jesus, there is no sin too great to be forgiven. The consequences for an intentional sin are a reality, but if one seeks a right heart attitude in faith toward God, He promises forgiveness and may intervene in the consequences.

Questions for Pondering

Am I experiencing God's peace in my life?

If I do not have peace, do I need to check my heart attitude for

- unconfessed sins,
- unforgiveness, and
- misplaced priorities?

Chapter 45

What Is on Your Table?

> You prepare a table before me in the presence of my enemies; you anoint my head with oil; my cup overflows. (Psalm 23:5)

During a discussion group, Psalm 23:5 was mentioned followed by a very thought-provoking question: If the Lord is preparing a table for you, what exactly is on your table? A number of typical answers were presented, itemizing all sorts of banquet delicacies. Then one man, noted for his passion for studying the Bible, chimed in that he knew exactly what would be on his table and it would not be food. That piqued everyone's curiosity! He proceeded to explain that what he wanted would be a table piled high with books, parchments, and scrolls containing the answers and insights to the many questions he had concerning the Word of God. Further, he expected he would have the peace and quiet necessary for him to study them even though his enemies would be present. He figured that since the context of the psalm was the Lord's blessing and provision, then the presence of his enemies would imply that they were subdued or prevented from harming or harassing him in any way.

This was quite an unexpected answer to the proposed discussion question. It proved to be an intriguing question and answer for all in the room.

Another possibility that came to light was that what lay on the table might be a list of the tasks the Lord has prepared for us to accomplish in our lives as He did for Saul of Tarsus in Acts 9:16.

Lesson

This psalm presents several statements that give rise to thought-provoking questions when we think outside the box.

Questions for Pondering

What would you want to be on the table the Lord is preparing for you?

If my enemies are here in my presence, what are they doing?

Am I expected to respond or take action in some way against these enemies?

What other questions might I discover from the other statements in this psalm?

Chapter 46

The Power Jesus Gave

> And he called to him his twelve disciples and gave them authority over unclean spirits, to cast them out, and to heal every disease and every affliction. (Matthew 10:1)

This verse seems straightforward enough at first glance, but there is something odd in what Jesus did. He must have given the disciples power as the divine Son of God, not as a human being. As Jesus is our role model for how to walk in the Spirit here on earth, it must follow that all the miracles he accomplished were done in the power of the Holy Spirit and not as the divine Son. To do so as God and not human poses a problem for us: we cannot follow suit since we have no inherent power of our own to draw on. We must rely on the Holy Spirit as He demonstrated while living on earth.

We learn from the three following scriptures that the disciples were to wait for the empowerment of the Holy Spirit at Pentecost.:

> And I will ask the Father, and he will give you another Helper, to be with you forever. (John 14:16)

And behold, I am sending the promise of my Father upon you. But stay in the city until you are clothed with power from on high. (Luke 24:49)

But you will receive power when the Holy Spirit has come upon you, and you will be my witnesses in Jerusalem and in all Judea and Samaria, and to the end of the earth. (Acts 1:8)

Since the Holy Spirit had not yet come, the authority Jesus gave the disciples must have been His own. The Greek word for *authority* is *exousia*, which is translated variously *authority, jurisdiction, liberty, power, right*, or *strength*. In Luke 24:49 and Acts 1:8, the word used for power is *dynamis*—the power to perform miracles.

What Jesus did was to delegate authority to the disciples in a similar way authority is delegated to the police to enforce the laws of the land. This brings a whole new understanding to the statement in Matthew 28:18–20:

And Jesus came and said to them, "All authority in heaven and on earth has been given to me. Go therefore and make disciples of all nations, baptizing them in the name of the Father and of the Son and of the Holy Spirit, teaching them to observe all that I have commanded you. And behold, I am with you always, to the end of the age."

Since all authority has been given to Jesus, it follows that Jesus said that the Holy Spirit would not guide on the Holy Spirit's own authority.

When the Spirit of truth comes, he will guide you into all the truth, for he will not speak on his own authority, but whatever he hears he will speak, and he will declare to you the things that are to come. (John 16:13)

Lesson

It should be sobering to realize the magnitude of the responsibility, as well as the privilege, that has been given to the believer. This authority included the power of life and death, as we observe it was wielded by the prophets of old. James and John had the power but would have misused it.

> And when his disciples James and John saw it, they said, "Lord, do you want us to tell fire to come down from heaven and consume them?" But he turned and rebuked them. (Luke 9:54ff)

If they did not have the power, there would be no need to rebuke them.

Question for Pondering

Consider the privilege and responsibility I have by being given the name of Jesus for the work of the kingdom. Remember death and life are in the power of the tongue (Proverbs 18:21).

Chapter 47

Take and Show?

All that the Father has is mine; therefore, I said that he
will take what is mine and declare it to you. (John 16:15)

This is an unusual and intriguing statement in light of Colossians 1:16:

> For by him all things were created, in heaven and
> on earth, visible and invisible, whether thrones or
> dominions or rulers or authorities—all things were
> created through him and for him.

This passage clearly states that everything was created by and
for Him. Just what then is the Father's? At first glance, this seems
perplexing. However, this passage does not say that He owns it; only
that Christ created it. The Father's will may have been for Christ to
bring all things into existence for the purpose of making a world
ready for the incarnation and birth of Jesus. That would make the
"for Him" statement above much more amazing. This would also
be in keeping with the apostle Paul's observation that God's plan of
salvation was made before the foundation of the world:

Blessed be the God and Father of our Lord Jesus Christ, who has blessed us in Christ with every spiritual blessing in the heavenly places, even as he chose us in him before the foundation of the world, that we should be holy and blameless before him. (Ephesians 1:3ff)

Also consider 1 Corinthians 15:27ff: "For God 'has put all things in subjection under his feet.'" But when it says "all things in subjection," it is plain that He is excepted as He who put all things in subjection under Him. When all things are subjected to Him, then the Son Himself will also be subjected to Him who put all things in subjection under Him, that God may be all in all.

Here we see the cycle complete. The Father has given Jesus Christ all things so that, at the end of all history, Jesus will lay it all at the feet of the Father. Such is the relationship in the Godhead and the relationship we as believers have been invited to participate in.

So returning to John 16:15, we see the Holy Spirit is to declare or show us our heritage in Him, thus equipping us to stand against our enemy, Satan, with confidence. The Holy Spirit shows us that Jesus has gained the victory. As noted in Ephesians 1:3, we are blessed with all spiritual blessings. Having it is not the same as knowing that we have it. It lies with the Holy Spirit to show us what these blessings are. So we should take authority and stand in what is ours in Him.

Lesson

We have access to what Jesus has because He has delegated to us His authority, but we all too often are ignorant of what these blessings are apart from the Holy Spirit's activity.

Questions for Pondering

With authority comes responsibility. Have I avoided or am I avoiding responsibility to obey the Great Commission, which Jesus commanded all His people?

Do I believe I have the authority Jesus gave me? If not, what is causing me to doubt?

If the doubts come from teaching, which should I believe—what people teach or what the Bible says?

Chapter 48

When He Tells Us Plainly

I have said these things to you in figures of speech. The hour is coming when I will no longer speak to you in figures of speech but will tell you plainly about the Father. In that day you will ask in my name, and I do not say to you that I will ask the Father on your behalf; for the Father himself loves you, because you have loved me and have believed that I came from God. I came from the Father and have come into the world, and now I am leaving the world and going to the Father. (John 16:25–28)

Do we need to wait until we are in heaven with Him, or is the Holy Spirit giving us assurances now? It seems Jesus answers this question in John 16:12–14:

I still have many things to say to you, but you cannot bear them now. When the Spirit of truth comes, he will guide you into all the truth, for he will not speak on his own authority, but whatever he hears he will speak, and he will declare to you the things that are to come. He will glorify me, for he will take what is mine and declare it to you.

It could be that some of what He hears and speaks to the believer is what He hears Jesus revealing about the Father. What remains for the believer is to discern what new information the Holy Spirit has revealed. Just what is it that the disciples were not able to bear hearing prior to the resurrection? Clues may be found in what the apostle Paul taught about the Father, which was distinctly an addition to what Jesus taught during His earthly ministry.

Supremely, God is the Father of Jesus, the Son, who is loved:

He has delivered us from the domain of darkness and transferred us to the kingdom of his beloved Son, in whom we have redemption, the forgiveness of sins. (Colossians 1:13)

D. Guthrie and R. P. Martin summarize this difficult concept: "It is the divine purpose to replicate in the lives of Christ's people the image of his Son so that by the Spirit's ministry (2 Corinthians 3:18) the likeness of his Son is being made increasingly more apparent until at length, at the consummation of their salvation, they become "conformed to the image" of Christ (Romans 8:28).[14]" This concept was nearly impossible for the monotheistic first century Jewish mind as it is still for us today.

Jesus often talked about God as His Father, calling Him Abba. In this conversation and prayer, it is through the agency of the Spirit "by which believers come to this recognition and acclamation of God as one known and approached intimately. It is the mark of the 'spirit of sonship/adoption' that the Spirit places the seal of his witness on believers as sons/children of God, delivering them from nomistic religion with its uncertainty of God and pagan fearfulness that is, for Paul, akin to slavery."[15]

> For you did not receive the spirit of slavery to fall back into fear, but you have received the Spirit of adoption as sons, by whom we cry, "Abba! Father!" The Spirit himself bears witness with our spirit that we are children of God. (Romans 8:15–16)

> But when the fullness of time had come, God sent forth his Son, born of woman, born under the law, to redeem those who were under the law, so that we might receive adoption as sons. And because you are sons, God has sent the Spirit of his Son into our hearts, crying, "Abba! Father!" (Galatians 4:4–7)

Lesson

Prior to the resurrection, Jesus knew the disciples would be unable to accept what He wanted to tell them due to their cultural preconceptions. Even today it is difficult to understand that all believers would, through adoption, be participants in the divine community with all the rights and privileges of sonship. As we continue on our spiritual journeys, we encounter hard times and realizations we do not want to face. We may find ourselves in a place, as did the disciples, faced with realizations or memories that we are not ready to face or understand. We must ask the Holy Spirit, our Comforter, to guide us through these sensitive areas.

Questions for Pondering

What are you not prepared to hear?

- Future death of a loved one?
- Future economic problems, hardship, or loss?
- Future political uncertainty?
- Future physical health change?

What is a legalistic mind not capable of understanding?

Chapter 49

What about the Staff That Comforted?

> Even though I walk through the valley of the shadow
> of death, I will fear no evil, for you are with me; your
> rod and your staff, they comfort me. (Psalm 23:4)

What about the rod and staff that David references in this psalm gave him comfort? As discussed earlier, David took a staff along with a sling when he went out to face Goliath. In battle, a staff is used for defense, to block a blow, but also as an offensive weapon to strike out. However, its effectiveness depends upon the user's skill. If you do not have confidence in your own skill level, having a rod or staff may not give you comfort. However, David is not talking about his rod and staff but the LORD's. David may have had the rod and staff in mind as weapons, thinking about two scriptures.

He may have been remembering God as a warrior with consuming fire, as described by Moses.

Hear, O Israel: you are to cross over the Jordan today, to go in to dispossess nations greater and mightier than you, cities great and fortified up to heaven, a people great and tall, the sons of the Anakim, whom you know, and of whom you have heard it said, "Who can stand before the sons of Anak?" Know therefore today that he who goes over before you as a consuming fire is the Lord your God. He will destroy them and subdue them before you. So you shall drive them out and make them perish quickly, as the LORD has promised you. (Deuteronomy 9:1–3)

The author of Hebrews quotes the Old Testament, recalling that God is a consuming fire (Hebrews 12:28ff). Second, in Israel's more recent history, Judges 6:21 records an instance of God using His staff for the purpose of fire.

Then the Angel of the LORD reached out the tip of the staff that was in his hand and touched the meat and the unleavened cakes. And fire sprang up from the rock and consumed the meat and the unleavened cakes. And the angel of the LORD vanished from his sight.

There are two other aspects of how a rod and staff may be viewed. A rod is also used as a guidance tool to direct or guide a sheep to a destination. The pillar of fire was not only a guide for the people through the wilderness, giving light and warmth during the cold wilderness night, but also a defense against Pharaoh and his army at the Red Sea.

Fire may have been used as a warning to the people in Numbers 11:1ff:

> And the people complained in the hearing of the LORD about their misfortunes, and when the LORD heard it, his anger was kindled, and the fire of the LORD burned among them and consumed some outlying parts of the camp. Then the people cried out to Moses, and Moses prayed to the LORD, and the fire died down.

Upon close inspection, the text does not say people died, but fire sprang up among them as well as outside the camp and then died down. No people are recorded as being killed.

The second use of a staff is as a means for rest. While on a long hike, the hiker can lean on a staff for a momentary break, relieving the load of the backpack.

Lesson

To get comfort from God, it is important to get into the Word of God. It is the key source, reminding us of His faithfulness and promises. Seek His wisdom and guidance.

> Trust in the LORD with all your heart, and do not lean on your own understanding. In all your ways acknowledge him, and he will make straight your paths. (Proverbs 3:5ff)

Questions for Pondering

When I am going through a trial or hard time, do I trust in His faithfulness?

Do I have a good understanding of scripture so as to gain comfort in what it tells me of who and whose I am?

In times of trouble, do I encourage myself by bringing to mind His promises made to me in scripture?

Chapter 50

Where Was the Samaritan Leper Going?

When he saw them he said to them, "Go and show yourselves to the priests." And as they went they were cleansed. (Luke 17:14–16)

Samaritans were looked down upon because they were considered half breeds; they were the Jews who were not taken into Babylonian captivity and married into the indigenous populations. Although they observed the Torah, they were not strict in its observance. One deviation was that they considered Mt. Gerizim as holy and worshiped there rather than at Jerusalem. As a result, they had their own priesthood not located in Jerusalem. It is likely that the Samaritan was taking a different path on his way to show himself to the priests at Mt. Gerizim, rather than in Jerusalem. When the Samaritan leper realized that he was healed, he returned to thank Jesus. For this man, thankfulness was more important than obedience to the letter of the law.

Lesson

When the Lord asks you to do something, the important point is the obedience. It is the response and doing it to the best of your ability and knowledge that matters.

Questions for Pondering

Do I let public opinion or social taboos interfere with my obedience in doing what God is asking me to do?

Jesus said that, if we love Him, we must obey what He taught. How well am I doing in my obedience?

> If you love Me, you will keep my commandments. (John 14:15)

Chapter 51

What Might Have Been: Twenty-Twenty Hindsight

Then she arose with her daughters-in-law to return from the country of Moab, for she had heard in the fields of Moab that the LORD had visited his people and given them food. So she set out from the place where she was with her two daughters-in-law, and they went on the way to return to the land of Judah. But Naomi said to her two daughters-in-law, "Go, return each of you to her mother's house. May the LORD deal kindly with you, as you have dealt with the dead and with me. The LORD grant that you may find rest, each of you in the house of her husband!" Then she kissed them, and they lifted up their voices and wept. And they said to her, "No, we will return with you to your people." But Naomi said, "Turn back, my daughters; why will you go with me? Have I yet sons in my womb that they may become your husbands?" (Ruth 1:6–11)

In this passage, we see that Naomi is destitute and in despair. With her personal tragedies and without hope, she has lost sight of the LORD as her provider. She has also forgotten God's provision of the levirate marriage:

> If brothers dwell together, and one of them dies and has no son, the wife of the dead man shall not be married outside the family to a stranger. Her husband's brother shall go in to her and take her as his wife and perform the duty of a husband's brother to her. And the first son whom she bears shall succeed to the name of his dead brother, that his name may not be blotted out of Israel. And if the man does not wish to take his brother's wife, then his brother's wife shall go up to the gate to the elders and say, "My husband's brother refuses to perpetuate his brother's name in Israel; he will not perform the duty of a husband's brother to me." Then the elders of his city shall call him and speak to him, and if he persists, saying, "I do not wish to take her," then his brother's wife shall go up to him in the presence of the elders and pull his sandal off his foot and spit in his face. And she shall answer and say, "So shall it be done to the man who does not build up his brother's house." (Deuteronomy 25:5–9)

It is apparent that Naomi and her family followed the LORD on two counts:

- Naomi blesses her daughters-in-law by the name of the LORD.
- Ruth professes that Naomi's people and God shall be hers as well, rejecting the god of Moab. She invokes a curse upon herself in the name of the LORD.

But Ruth said, "Do not urge me to leave you or to return from following you. For where you go I will go, and where you lodge I will lodge. Your people shall be my people, and your God my God. Where you die I will die, and there will I be buried. May the LORD do so to me and more also if anything but death parts me from you." (Ruth 1:16–17)

Ruth proclaims her love and devotion to both Naomi and the God of Israel. She confirms her statements as true and sincere by taking an oath. Because of this oath, Naomi ceases urging Ruth to turn back to Moab as Orpah has done. Orpah was convinced by Naomi's despairing logic; not willing to face the unknown risk by faith, she returns to her home in Moab.

The speculation in this story stems from the name order that is used for the various people in the story. In Ruth 1:2, the sons are listed. Later, the sons marry, and their wives' names are listed. In general, children's names are recited in birth order, even today. If this is the case here, it logically follows that Orpah, who is listed first, is the wife of the firstborn, followed by Ruth, who married the second-born.

Later in Ruth's story, Boaz agrees to marry Ruth as her kinsman redeemer, following the levirate law quoted above, but he must go to the next person in line who has this obligation. We see this recorded in Ruth 3:12ff and Ruth 4:1–5. If the assumption about birth order is correct, then this man, who was first in line, would have been the kinsman redeemer for Orpah, as the wife of the firstborn.

Lesson

God's provision often takes many unexpected forms. Ruth chose to follow Naomi out of love and devotion. It is likely that all three women were unaware of the levirate law provision. Ruth's choice was a step of faith in a new beginning, not knowing precisely what events would transpire. She stepped out in faith, and God's provision blessed her beyond her wildest dreams at that moment. Orpah did not, deciding instead to play it safe by returning to what she knew, and thus lost God's great provision for her.

Question for Pondering

In times of difficulty, are my decisions ruled by the risks I perceive or by faith, trusting in what He has told me in His Word?

Sometimes it feels safer to endure the pain I know than the pain, real or feared, in choosing a path that may result in my freedom or healing.

Chapter 52

What about Tasteless Salt?

> You are the salt of the earth, but if salt has lost its taste, how shall its saltiness be restored? It is no longer good for anything except to be thrown out and trampled under people's feet. (Matthew 5:13)

Have you ever wondered how salt could lose its flavor? Since pure salt cannot lose its taste, it follows that the salt discussed here is contaminated with gypsum or some form of lime. The entry for *salt* in the *Greek-English Lexicon of the New Testament Based on Semantic Domains* reads as follows:

> Since salt is a universal condiment, there is no difficulty involved in finding an adequate expression for it, but there is a difficulty in Matthew 5:13. In the ancient world, however, what was often sold as salt was highly adulterated and the sodium chloride could leach out in humid weather, in which case the residue (normally a form of lime) would be useless.

Vincent's Word Studies in the New Testament relates the following story[16]:

> Dr. Thompson ("the Land and the Book") cites the following case: "a merchant of Sidon, having farmed of the government the revenue from the importation of salt, brought over a great quantity from the marshes of Cyprus—enough, in fact, to supply the whole province for many years. This he had transferred to the mountains, to cheat the government out of some small percentage of duty. Sixty-five houses were rented and filled with salt. Such houses have merely earth floors, and the salt next to the ground was in a few years entirely spoiled. I saw large quantities of it literally thrown into the road to be trodden under foot of men and beast. It was 'good for nothing.'"

With all the salt leached out, the residue, which was formerly "salt," had lost its flavor. The area around the Dead Sea in Israel has extremely low humidity. The Dead Sea salt is sold for mineral bath treatments. A sealed container of this salt, once opened in a more humid location, will have water forming in the container over the course of a week or two.

Lesson

In the above story, the salt from Cyprus was contaminated, either from impurities in the marsh salt deposit or from being adulterated by a dishonest merchant. If the salt and contaminant are each considered as a master in its own pure form, Jesus' comment in Matthew 6:24 is insightful:

No one can serve two masters, for either he will hate the one and love the other, or he will be devoted to the one and despise the other. You cannot serve God and money.

Questions for Pondering

We live in a very contaminated world by God's standards.

- When was the last time I took stock of how much "worldly contamination" is in my life?
- How much integrity of character do I have? Stated a different way, am I living a double standard?
  - Do I live differently on Sunday than the rest of the week?
  - Do I live differently at work versus at home?
  - Do I live differently when with friends than when with someone of the opposite gender?

Chapter 53

The Prodigal in Place

Let's look at the older son in the Prodigal Son story.

> Now his older son was in the field, and as he came and drew near to the house, he heard music and dancing. And he called one of the servants and asked what these things meant. And he said to him, "Your brother has come, and your father has killed the fattened calf, because he has received him back safe and sound." But he was angry and refused to go in. His father came out and entreated him, but he answered his father, "Look, these many years I have served you, and I never disobeyed your command, yet you never gave me a young goat, that I might celebrate with my friends. But when this son of yours came, who has devoured your property with prostitutes, you killed the fattened calf for him!" And he said to him, "Son, you are always with me, and all that is mine is yours. It was fitting to celebrate and be glad, for this your brother was dead, and is alive; he was lost, and is found." (Luke 15:25–32)

In Jewish tradition, this parable is known as the parable of the two sons. It is the last is a series of parables related to address Scribes' and Pharisees' criticism for receiving sinners. Yet the parable is not directed against them since they agree with the premise. The parable is about a Father's response to his two sons. We are familiar with the part concerning the prodigal son who left, but what about the other prodigal — "the prodigal in place"? Why is the elder son a prodigal? Let's look at the various issues that are hinted at in the text of Luke 15:25–32.

1. First, the elder son is self-centered. He is angry and resentful since his father never gave him a fattened calf to "celebrate with my friends." He also possibly resents his father for exercising his usufructive[17] right to spend his money to celebrate the brother's return. In the Mishnaic tractate *Baba Bathra*, the law states, "If a man assigned his goods to his son to be his after his death, the father cannot sell them since they are assigned to his son, and the son cannot sell them because they are in the father's control. If the father sold them, they are sold only until he dies; if the son sold them, the buyer has no claim on them until the father dies."[18]

2. Second, he has no love for his brother since he uses the phrase "this son of yours."

3. Third, he is irresponsible. According to Middle Eastern culture and Jewish traditional values, the elder son would hold the position of mediator in a family crisis. He has neglected his duty as eldest son by his silence on the matter of his brother leaving with a third of the estate.

4. Fourth, he also has a broken relationship with his father; he fails to address his father with a title of honor. Added to that,

he treats his father as an employer, obeying out of obligation rather than out of love.

5. Last, he is humiliating his father and insulting the guests. In Semitic culture, failing to be present for the celebration, without good reason, was not only disrespectful but insulting. Note David's absence at King Saul's dinner table (1 Samuel 20:5ff):

> David said to Jonathan, "Behold, tomorrow is the new moon, and I should not fail to sit at table with the king. But let me go, that I may hide myself in the field till the third day at evening. If your father misses me at all, then say, 'David earnestly asked leave of me to run to Bethlehem his city, for there is a yearly sacrifice there for all the clan.'"

Here David is obligated to attend the king's feast and sends a solid reason via his covenantal friend Jonathan.

Lesson

A rabbinic parable parallels the prodigal parable.[19] Here the father (Abba) pleads with his son not to leave home: "Do not be ashamed to return to me." In rabbinic thought, it is never too late for the sinner to repent and receive divine compassion. The rabbinic parables, like the illustration of the prodigal son, are filled with the great imagery of divine mercy, which is always bestowed on the person who truly repents.[20]

Questions for Pondering

There is *more to the story*. In telling this parable, Jesus stops short in relating what the older son's response is. The unspoken expectation is that I am invited to step up onto the stage and pick up the role of the elder son. If I can be truly honest with myself and God the Father, which path will I choose?

1. Recognize my dysfunction, in whatever area; repent; and be restored into right relationship with the Father; or
2. Fail to recognize the area(s) of dysfunctionality in my life, and try to live apart from a sold-out loving relationship with the Father.

Chapter 54

Angelic Assumptions

Have you ever wondered about the assumptions we make regarding scripture? Many of these are based upon "a hear-say gospel" or traditions. Often these come about because we find ourselves too busy to stop and verify, "Did the Bible really say that?" A couple of these are related to what we know and do not know about angels.

Assumption 1: All angels have wings.

On checking out scriptural references to angels, it appears that people saw angels on several occasions. Some examples are Abraham, Lot and the residence of Sodom, Samson's parents, Elisha (after the victory on Mt. Carmel), David at the threshing floor of Ornan, shepherds watching their flock by night, Peter while in prison, Philip told to go to the Ethiopian Eunuch, and Cornelius the centurion. In all these instances, no mention is made to their having wings, and in some cases the observers did not recognize them as angels. Often, the angels are depicted with wings as in the tabernacle curtains and the mercy seat on the ark of the covenant.

One possibility is that the angels, being spirit beings, can take on any form.

> And no wonder, for even Satan disguises himself as an angel of light. (2 Corinthians 11:14)

The chosen form could be with or without wings, or perhaps they had wings and were recognized as angels, so there was no need to comment on them. Often the observers sensed their holiness or recognized them because of the attendant light. The latter would be the reason for the comment that Steven's face was like that of an angel (Acts 6:15).

Assumption 2: Angels sing.

In many of our traditional Christmas carols, the lyrics proclaim angels singing a chorus. On closer examination, the text simply states that the angels were praising God and "saying" (Luke 2:13). In all instances, angels simply speak. There does not seem to be any text stating that angels sing. Singing in the New Testament Greek culture entails people speaking in unison as a group. Speaking to a melody, such as in Jewish worship or as we define singing today, was a foreign concept to the Greeks. One school of thought is that singing and creating music are part of humankind being created in the image of God. The Bible is silent on whether angels were created in God's image or imbued with the ability to create, such as art or music.

Assumption 3: Angels feel joy.

"I tell you, there is joy before the angels of God over one sinner who repents" (Luke 15:10). The use of the word *before* in this verse is interesting. The question is, who has the joy? It could mean the joy of the Lord that the angels behold, or it could be the angel's joy in beholding the event. If it is the latter, then there is an interesting rhetorical question that comes to mind: Do the angels look forward in anticipation to having fellowship with the saints in heaven along with Jesus?

Lesson

There is no substitute for reading the Bible for yourself, not depending on a hear-say gospel or opinion.

Questions for Pondering

It is my sincere prayer that these articles have been not only entertaining but thought provoking. I hope you begin to ask questions of the text when reading the Word of God. Three helpful questions in undertaking biblical study are

- What does the text say?
- What does the text mean to the audience? and
- What does the text mean to me?

The rest of the story is to be discovered by you, as you become aware of the assumptions you bring to the text. When you read or hear God's Word, ask questions:

- Why is this detail here?
- Why is it important?
- Where is this place name relative to the preceding or following text?

About the cover: The Torah scroll is opened to the Shammah, Deuteronomy 6:4, and laying on a traditional prayer shawl. The pointer or *etsbah* (finger) pointing to the tetra gram name of God is of Persian origin. The gems in the handle are likely rubies.

Endnotes

1   W. Gunther Plaut, ed., *The Torah: A Modern Commentary* (New York: Union of American Hebrew Congregations, 1981), 415.

2   D. R. W. Wood, *New Bible Dictionary, Third Edition* (Downers Grove: IVP, 2004), 682.

3   William Smith, *Dr. William Smith's Dictionary of the Bible* (Grand Rapids: Baker Book House, 1971), 1627

4   For a nonmathematical explanation in layperson terms, see Jim Al-Khalili, *Quantum: A Guide for the Perplexed* (London: Weidenfeld & Nicolson).

5   William Smith, *Smith's Bible Dictionary*, reproduced in Libronix Bible Reference Library [CD-ROM] (Nashville: Thomas Nelson, 1997), 139.

6   Wood, *New Bible Dictionary*, 446.

7   Justo L. González, *The Story of Christianity vol 1* (Harper San Francisco, 1984), 94.

8   Authorship disputed.

9   The original Hebrew text of 2 Kings 2:23 implies that these were young adolescents since young children would likely not be outside the city walls because of the danger of wild animals. Also, the bears mauled but did not kill the boys.

10   In the Greek, the "Him" is implied and often translated "Christ" but could also, refer to the Holy Spirit.

11   Lanny and Marilyn Johnson, "The Crimson or Scarlet Worm," Alpha Omega Institute, http://www.discovercreation.org/blog/2011/11/20/the-crimson-or-scarlet-worm/ 12/6/2017

12   *Merriam-Webster's Collegiate Dictionary*, Eleventh Edition (Springfield, MA: Merriam-Webster Inc., 2003), 1455.

13   A. W Tozer, *The Pursuit of God* (Camp Hill, PA: Christian Publications Inc., 1982).

14 Gerald F. Hawthorne and Ralph P. Martin, eds., *Dictionary of Paul and His Letters* (Downers Grove: IVP, 1993) 358.

15 Ibid.

16 Marvin R. Vincent, McDonald Publishing Company McLean, Virginia 1984 vol 1 p 38, Quoted from Thomson, William M., *The Land and the Book.* New York, 1880–86. Quoted in *The Parables: Jewish Tradition and Christian Interpretation* (199811), 185.

17 The legal right of using and enjoying the fruits or profits of something belonging to another. (*Merriam-Webster's Collegiate Dictionary*) 1379.

18 M. B. Bat. 8:7 (*Mishnah,* ed. Albeck, 146; trans. Fanby, *Mishnah,* 376); cf. b. *B. Bat.* 136a. See also, Sir 33:19–23; b. *B. Metzia* 75b.

19 *Pesiq. Rab.*44 (*Pesikta Rabbati,* ed. Friedmann, 184b–185a). Quoted in *The Parables: Jewish Tradition and Christian Interpretation* (1998), 151. See the translation by W. Braude, *Pesikta Rabbati* (2 vols.: New Haven: Yale University Press, 1968), 2:779.

20 Brad H. Young, *The Parables: Jewish Tradition and Christian Interpretation* (Hendrickson Publishers, LLC, 118), 152.

Index

J

James
    1:12 131
Jeremiah
    9:24 87
    29:11 7
    31:33 15
Job
    35:1 98
    39:5 33
    40:9 123
    42:7 99
John
    1:1-3 24
    1:12 15
    2:3-10 76
    3:3 15
    3:16 121
    3:35 94, 95
    5:19 75
    7:1 91
    9:39 96
    10:30 2
    12:28f 126
    12:49 75
    14:13 39
    14:15 39, 168
    14:16 72, 153
    14:26 72, 110
    15:1 117
    15:7 58
    15:9 58
    15:13 3
    15:15 1

    16:12 159
    16:13 154
    16:15 156, 157
    16:23f 104
    16:25 159
    17 75
    17:9 102
    17:15 102
    17:20 102
    19:25 90
Judges
    6:21 164
    14:4 55, 82
    14:6 81
    14:19 82

L

Leviticus
    7:19 67
Luke
    1:19f 146
    2:13 181
    4:22 37
    5:4ff 79
    6:38 73, 135, 136
    8:27 79
    9:54f 155
    11:20 79
    15:10 181
    15:25 176, 177
    17:14 167
    20:34 84
    22:31 103
    24:49 154

R

Revelation
- 3:11 132
- 4:10 131
- 6:11 107
- 7:14 18, 107
- 10:4 125
- 11:19 17
- 12:12 147
- 13:8 4
- 14:14 131
- 20:12 9
- 21:1 84

Romans
- 1:17 44
- 8:15 161
- 8:28 160
- 8:31 102
- 12:2 2

Ruth
- 1:6-11 169
- 1:16 171
- 3:12f 171
- 4:1 171

Z

Zechariah
- 1:12 145, 146